FAMOUS INDIAN CHIEFS
I HAVE KNOWN

B270   Animalia by Graeme Base © Harry N. Abrams. Inc. 1986

"For many months there were battles—battles—battles!"

FAMOUS INDIAN CHIEFS
I HAVE KNOWN

BY
MAJOR-GENERAL O. O. HOWARD
U. S. ARMY

WITH ILLUSTRATIONS BY
GEORGE VARIAN

Introduction by Bruce J. Dinges

University of Nebraska Press
Lincoln and London

The paper used in this publication meets the minimum re-
quirements of the American National Standard for Informa-
tion Sciences—Permanence of Paper for Printed Library
Materials, ANSI Z239.48-1984.

First Bison Book printing: 1989
Most recent printing indicated by the first digit below:
1 2 3 4 5 6 7 8 9 10

Library of Congress Cataloging-in-Publication Data
Howard, O. O. (Oliver Otis), 1830–1909.
Famous Indian chiefs I have known / by O. O. Howard; with
illustrations by George Varian; introduction by Bruce J.
Dinges.
p.   cm.
Reprint. Originally published: New York: Century Co., 1908.
"Bison."
Bibliography: p.
ISBN 0-8032-2350-1.   ISBN 0-8032-7241-3 (pbk.)
1. Indians of North America—Biography.   I. Varian,
George.   II. Title.
E89.H69   1989   88-20756
970.00497022—dc19   CIP
[B]

Reprinted from the 1908 edition published by the Century
Company, New York

CONTENTS

CONTENTS

LIST OF ILLUSTRATIONS

LIST OF ILLUSTRATIONS

INTRODUCTION
By Bruce J. Dinges

Beginning with the November 1907 issue and conclud-
ing in October 1908, *St. Nicholas* magazine carried a se-
ries of notable articles by retired Major General O. O.
Howard. Written for young readers and illustrated by the
popular artist George Varian, they were simple stories of
the author's personal acquaintance with some of the most
prominent Indian leaders of the nineteenth century. And
they offered more than mere diversion. "Probably no white
man," the magazine's editor remarked, "has ever known
so many Indian Chiefs as General Howard." Howard, whose
military career spanned four decades, was a friend and
supporter of the American Indian long before sentimen-
talists concocted the image of the noble red man. When
his stories reappeared as *Famous Indian Chiefs I Have
Known*,[1] they provided a generation of readers with a
positive image of Native Americans far different from the
brutal stereotypes that had prevailed less than a generation earlier. For today's reader, Howard's engaging book
is a valuable historical document and a classic expression
of turn-of-the-century liberal thought on the Indian question. Out of print and all but forgotten since its original
publication eighty years ago, it has long deserved the new
lease on life that this Bison reprint will provide.

INTRODUCTION

As a child, Oliver Otis Howard ("Otis" to his family and friends) listened with fascination and horror to his grandfather's stories of Indian atrocities and savage battles against the Tories and their Indian allies during the Revolutionary War. For years nightmares born of those tales told by flickering candlelight tormented his dreams. It could not have occurred to him that he would one day conduct his own Indian campaigns or that his sympathetic views toward the Indian would earn him a prominent place among those army officers who have come to be known as the humanitarian generals.

Although he achieved high rank, Howard's military career was hardly spectacular. Born in Leeds, Maine, on November 3, 1830, he graduated from Bowdoin College and stood fourth in the class of 1854 at the U.S. Military Academy. After tours of duty as an ordnance officer in Maine and Florida, he returned to West Point as an instructor of mathematics. In the meantime, he had married Elizabeth Ann Waite and fathered three children. Eventually, the Howards would raise five sons and two daughters.

A man of profound religious conviction, Howard was contemplating entering the ministry when the Civil War broke out. Putting his plans on hold, he fought as colonel of the Third Maine Infantry at the battle of First Bull Run. Thereafter he climbed rapidly in rank, primarily because of his connections with powerful Maine politicians. Promoted to brigadier general in September 1862 and to major general seven months later, he played a controversial role in several important battles in the Eastern Theater. At both Chancellorsville and Gettysburg, the German soldiers of his XI Corps broke under Confederate assaults. Transferred to the West, Howard redeemed himself as a skillful commander under General William T. Sherman. A mere first lieutenant at the outbreak of the war, Howard emerged from the conflict as a full-fledged

INTRODUCTION

brigadier general in the regular army. He was only thirty-five years old.

Howard's popular image is that of a stern, bearded figure in dress uniform. His right sleeve, empty since the amputation of his arm after the battle of Fair Oaks in 1862, is pinned to his frock coat. His left hand clutches a Bible.

Even in an age more openly religious than our own, Howard was widely known as the "Christian soldier," or the "praying general." His deep-seated piety and all-encompassing faith gave him courage and resolve that bordered on self-righteousness, providing at the same time a source of annoyance for some of his more worldly comrades. That courage and a belief that every soul was valuable in the sight of the Lord formed the bedrock of Howard's lifelong crusade to uplift the downtrodden and disadvantaged.

During his long and productive life, Howard had abundant opportunity to translate his humanitarian impulses into effective action. As commissioner of the Bureau of Refugees, Freedmen and Abandoned Lands (Freedmen's Bureau) from 1865 to 1872, he protected the rights of southern blacks as he helped them make the difficult transition from slavery to freedom. A fervent proponent of Negro education, he played an important role in the founding of Howard University in Washington, D.C., where he was president from 1869 until 1874. Later, he helped establish Lincoln University for disadvantaged whites in eastern Tennessee.

Even while he wrestled with the burdensome problems of the newly freed slaves, Howard turned his attention to another oppressed group, the Indian tribes of the trans-Mississippi West. In 1872 President Ulysses S. Grant temporarily relieved Howard of his duties with the Freedmen's Bureau and dispatched him on a mission to arrange peace between warring Indians and whites in the South-west. Amid a barrage of abuse from civilians and his fellow army officers, Howard concluded an agreement with the Chiricahua leader Cochise that ended more than a decade of bloodshed. Others had paved the way for Howard's success, but his courage in riding virtually alone and unarmed into Cochise's stronghold was remarkable. When he later wrote of the episode, he charitably bestowed the lion's share of the credit for Cochise's surrender on his guide, Tom Jeffords.

Ironically, the surrender of Cochise proved to be the crowning achievement in what would be more than a decade of service among the western tribes. As military commander in the Pacific Northwest from 1874 to 1880, Howard failed in his earnest efforts to prevent an armed confrontation between whites and the nontreaty Nez Perces, who were being driven off their land. He suffered further humiliation in the ensuing military campaign as the press and his army superiors bristled at the soldiers' inability to catch up with Chief Joseph's people during a thousand-mile race for the Canadian border. When the Indians were finally cut off just short of their goal, credit for Chief Joseph's surrender went to Colonel Nelson A. Miles, who had only lately taken up the pursuit. Howard performed more creditably in the Bannock-Paiute War of 1878 and the subsequent Sheepeater conflict, but for a man of his pride and ambition, the Nez Perce campaign was a source of deep bitterness and embarassment.

The remainder of Howard's military career was prosaic. He served briefly as superintendent of the military academy, then went on to command the Department of the Platte and, finally, the Military Division of the Atlantic. Promoted to major general in 1886, he was the army's second-highest-ranking officer when he retired in 1894 after forty-four years of active service. Settling at Burlington, Vermont, he devoted the remainder of his life to writing, lecturing, Republican politics, education, and

INTRODUCTION

Christian endeavors until his death on October 26, 1909, just short of his seventy-ninth birthday.[2]

In addition to his many other accomplishments, Howard was a gifted and prolific author. He embarked on his literary career partly out of necessity when his numerous philanthropic causes, and legal fees arising from court cases that alleged mismanagement and fraud in his administration of the Freedmen's Bureau, threatened him with impoverishment. Howard became a frequent contributor to national periodicals, and beginning about 1880 he produced nearly a dozen volumes of biography, reminiscences, and juvenile literature. His most important works include a two-volume autobiography published in 1907 and three books relating to his dealings with Indians—*Nez Perce Joseph* (1881), *My Life and Experiences among Our Hostile Indians* (1907), and *Famous Indian Chiefs I Have Known* (1908).

In his autobiographical writings, Howard attempted to alert people in the East to injustices perpetrated against the western tribes. Like most of his contemporaries, Howard believed that societies naturally progressed from barbarism to civilization and that so-called savage races must give way to the inexorable march of Anglo-Christian culture. But although he never for a moment doubted the eventual outcome of the struggle between whites and Indians, he opposed extermination and questioned the morality of depriving Indians of their lands.

From his personal experience, Howard was convinced that blame for much of the Indian problem lay not with the Indian but rather with the "equal or greater sinfulness of the Anglo-Saxon." In his estimation, the root cause of Indian wars could be found in "the refusal of whites to recognize Indian occupancy of land." Time after time, Howard had watched the government conclude treaties reserving for Indians vast acres, which avaricious settlers then stole through force or legal maneuver. Robbed of their hunting grounds and faced with starvation, Indians had little choice but to resort to violence.

Under these circumstances, it is not surprising that Howard opposed the government's policy of settling Indians on reservations, where presumably they would be fed and protected. To beat the Indians into submission and then follow defeat with slow starvation on a reservation struck Howard as cruel and counterproductive. In his view, it could only end in failure. He argued, along with the framers of the Dawes Act (1887), that Indians should be given title to individual tracts of land, where their rights would be protected by law and where they would be compelled to become self-sufficient.

Like most nineteenth-century reformers, Howard believed that the Indian problem would be solved only when Indians ceased to be Indian and were absorbed into the mainstream of American life and culture. Because the ties of tribal culture were strong, he doubted that adult Indians could ever live like whites. Convinced that the quickest and surest road to civilization was through education, Howard was a strong advocate of schools such as Hampton Institute and Carlisle, where Indian children could be removed from the "degrading influences" of their tribal surroundings and taught the white man's ways.[3]

In *Famous Indian Chiefs I Have Known,* Howard (with the help of his daughter-in-law Mrs. Harry S. Howard) describes for young readers his important role in Indian affairs. Along the way, he tries to teach a moral lesson: that Christianity and assimilation are the only roads to salvation for the Indians. To the extent that these sketches of twenty-three Indian leaders are presented with sympathy and understanding, his book is a yardstick showing how much attitudes had changed in the two decades since the closing of the frontier. Already the West and its Indian wars had entered the realm of myth. The great warriors Sitting Bull, Chief Joseph, and Cochise were dead and

INTRODUCTION

others like Red Cloud and Geronimo would join them (along with Howard) within a year of the book's publication.

Howard was an important link to that fading frontier past. During his long career, he probably had more and closer contact with tribes from Florida to Arizona and from Oregon to Alaska than any other officer in the U.S. army. He was unusual insofar as he listened patiently to their complaints, took pity on their plight, and devoted much serious thought to formulating just and humane solutions to what appeared to be almost insurmountable differences between whites and Indians. In his book he tells us how he labored to guide Indians to accept Anglo customs and practices.

It is obvious at once that Howard, who had written two previous juvenile books (*Donald's School Days* and *Henry in the War*), was a talented writer and entertaining storyteller, with a wry sense of humor. Writing from personal experience, he created engaging portraits—almost unheard of in his day—of Indians as flesh-and-blood human beings with a diverse range of personalities. Because of the cultural blinders he wore, Howard sometimes misjudged Indian motivations, but he left for the rest of us vivid descriptions of their physical appearance, demeanor, thoughts, and conversation.

For all his noble impulses, Howard was a captive of the time and culture in which he lived, and like most idealists he was capable of interpreting actions and events to fit his vision of a just society. An obvious example is the case of the sick and broken Apache leader Geronimo, who sadly had outlived his time and was reduced to a sideshow attraction. The cruel irony was lost on Howard, who could only marvel that "since he [Geronimo] had become a Christian he was trying to understand our civilization and, at last, after many years, Geronimo, the last Apache chief, was happy and joyful, for he had learned to try and be good to everybody and to love his white brothers."

INTRODUCTION

On other occasions, Howard could be quite astute, as with the great Sioux war leader Red Cloud, who continued to resist the imposition of Anglo culture long after he had laid down his weapons. Finally, when he was past eighty years of age and infirm, even this most intransigent of enemies conceded that "Indians must take land like white men, they must work with a plow and hoe, and they must read books and study." "Then," Howard noted perceptively, "there was peace in the north land, for the fiercest of all our Indian warriors had *really* [author's emphasis] surrendered."

On this level, *Famous Indian Chiefs I Have Known* is important for what it tells us about O. O. Howard and the aspirations of enlightened nineteenth-century Christian reformers for the Indian. Although Howard denigrated Indian culture, he accepted the basic humanity of Indians as souls to be won for Christ. He considered their struggle against the inroads of white civilization as doomed, but he realized that most often whites were responsible for initiating hostilities. And against long odds, he struggled mightily to save at least a remnant of the Indian people through education.

To the modern reader, Howard's attitudes toward Indians will seem ethnocentric, paternalistic, and even racist. But it would be unfair to measure him against twentieth-century values. By the standards of his time, Howard was a liberal thinker on the Indian question and his solutions were among the most enlightened that reformers of his day had to offer. It simply would not have occurred to him, or to any of his contemporaries, that there could be anything in Native American culture worth saving. At a time when some frontiersmen called loudly for extermination and the government sanctioned a policy of slow starvation on reservations, Indians found in Howard a benevolent friend, sympathetic listener, and strong voice for fairness, humanity, and justice. Nowhere are these

INTRODUCTION

qualities more plainly and eloquently stated than in *Famous Indian Chiefs I Have Known.*

NOTES

1. All of the material in *Famous Indian Chiefs I Have Known* appeared serially in *St. Nicholas* with the exception of "Mattie, The Daughter of Chief Shenkah" and "Chief Egan of the Malheurs." The magazine editors, on the other hand, augmented Howard's account of Sarah Winnemucca with an article entitled "Princess Sarah," by Colonel C. E. S. Wood (July 1908).

2. The standard biography is John A. Carpenter, *Sword and Olive Branch: Oliver Otis Howard* (University of Pittsburgh Press, 1964). William S. McFeely, *Yankee Stepfather: General O. O. Howard and the Freedmen* (New Haven: Yale University Press, 1968), measures Howard's activities as commissioner of the Freedmen's Bureau by a twentieth-century yardstick and, not surprisingly, concludes that by today's values he "failed the freedmen." For a useful corrective, see George C. Ruble's essay on Howard in Roger J. Spiller, ed., *Dictionary of American Military Biography*, 3 vols. (Westport, Conn.: Greenwood Press, 1984), vol. 2, pp. 493–96. Howard's role in Indian affairs has not been adequately explored. Robert M. Utley points the way in "Oliver Otis Howard," *New Mexico Historical Review* 62 (January 1987): 55–63. Interested students should first consult Richard N. Ellis's seminal article, "The Humanitarian Generals," *Western Historical Quarterly* 3 (April 1972): 169–78.

3. Howard's views on the Indian question are derived from O. O. Howard, *My Life and Experiences among Our Hostile Indians* (Hartford, Conn.: A. D. Worthington and Company, 1907).

FAMOUS INDIAN CHIEFS
I HAVE KNOWN

FAMOUS INDIAN CHIEFS
I HAVE KNOWN

I

OSCEOLA[1]

I SUSPECT "Uncle Sam" was born July
4th, 1776. If so, he was still a young man,
only twenty-eight years old, when Osceola
came into the world. The Red Stick tribe of
the Creek Indians had a camp on the bank of
the Chattahoochee. The water of this river
is colored by the roots of trees, shrubs, and
vines which grow along its sluggish current,

[1] Of course General Howard never saw Osceola, for he was
only a lad when the Seminole War was fought. But he
heard many vivid accounts, at the time, of the bravery and
skill of that fierce Indian warrior, and so a sketch of Osceola
fitly opens the book.—EDITOR.

and so it is very black. Osceola's mother, living near this dark river, named her baby Assa-he-ola,—black water. Spanish tongues by and by shortened it to the beautiful and Latin-like name of Osceola. Osceola's mother was the daughter of a Creek Indian chieftain. His father is said to have been an Indian trader born in England. There were three children, two girls and the boy. Osceola's mother, the proud and high-tempered Indian princess, became angry for some reason and taking her son went into the wilderness of southern Georgia and joined her own people, while the father took his two daughters and passed over to the far West. The princess taught Osceola both English and her own language, but she had come to hate the white people and did not fail to bring up her son with the same unkind feelings.

After a time troubles arose between our white settlers and the Creek Indians in Georgia, and Uncle Sam sent General Jackson with an army to drive the Indians further South.

At this time Osceola was only fourteen years old; yet he was so smart and so fierce that he became a leader of his people. Under him they fought hard, and were driven at last to the middle of Florida, where, not far from one of Uncle Sam's stockades, called Fort King, the tribe joined the Seminole Indians, who lived there. These Florida Indians, the Seminoles, were really a part of the Creek nation and spoke almost the same language. They soon became fond of Osceola, and as their head chief, Micanopy, was very old, in all fighting Osceola became the real leader. He had two under-chiefs, one named Jumper and the other Alligator. They were as fierce and hated the white people as much as he did, and enjoyed doing all he told them to do. As Osceola grew older he had a fine, manly bearing and a deep, soft, musical voice. He quickly learned a new language, and he was very skilful in the use of the bow, though he liked better the white man's rifle with powder and ball. It is said he always hit what he aimed at.

For fifteen years Osceola went from tribe to tribe and from chief to chief all over Florida and other states of the South, wherever he could find Indians. He always spoke against the white people, saying they were two-faced and would not treat the Indians with justice and mercy. I believe that Uncle Sam really had a good feeling for his red children; but the white people were very few in Florida, and they were afraid of the Indians and wanted to send them away to the West. So they asked Uncle Sam to send his officers and agents to make a bargain with the red-men. This bargain came about and was called the "Treaty of Payne's Landing." It was signed at Payne's Landing on the Ocklawaha

Osceola

River May 9, 1832, by some of the Indian chiefs and by Uncle Sam's white officers and agents. It was agreed that all the Indians were to go far away beyond the Mississippi River before the end of the year, and that Uncle Sam should give them $3000 each year and other things which were written in the treaty. Only a few of the Indians really agreed to go, and Osceola, now twenty-eight years old, was very much against giving away the Seminole country. He aroused the whole nation, nine tenths of the head men were with him, and he gathered good warriors, divided them into companies and drilled them. Osceola called an Indian assembly, and rising to his full height (5 feet 8 inches), took a strong bow in his right hand and an arrow in his left, and said, "I will not sign a treaty to give away the Indians' land, and I will kill the chiefs or any followers who sign it."

9

Two years passed, and then some Seminole chieftains, who had gone beyond the Mississippi, returned. They reported against the removal of the Indians, and the Indian Agent called a meeting of well-known Indians and white men to talk it over. The old chief, Micanopy, spoke for the Indians, but Osceola sat near and whispered into his ear what to answer the Indian Agent. Micanopy was old and wanted peace. He, Jumper, Alligator, and others said they never meant to sign away their land, but only agreed to send some men to look over the new country before they decided what to do. The meeting became very excited, and at last Osceola sprang to his feet and defied the agent, saying in a taunting manner, "Neither I nor my warriors care if we never receive another dollar from the Great Father." The agent, spreading the treaty upon the table, remonstrated with Osceola, but the fierce chief drew his long knife from its sheath and cried: "The only treaty I will execute is with this," and he drove the knife through and through the paper into the table.

Soon after this Osceola had an interview with Captain Ming of the Coast Survey near Fort King, but he declined every civility and said, "I will not break bread with a white man." A formal council was arranged, but here Osceola in a threatening manner seized a surveyor's chain and declared in a loud voice, "If you cross my land I will break this chain into as many pieces as there are links in it, and then throw the pieces so far you can never get them together again." The Indian Agent, in desperation, sent for Osceola and ordered him to sign the papers for transporting the Indians, but he answered, "I will not." When told that General Jackson, the President, would soon teach him better, Osceola replied, "I care no more for Jackson than for you."

11

The Indian Agent knowing that Osceola stirred up his people, had him put in prison at the fort, but he escaped by making promises to his guards. As soon as he was free again he began to get his warriors ready for battle. He went from place to place very fast, hardly stopping for food, till he had a large number of braves gathered near Fort King. Their knives were kept sharp, but sheathed, and rifles were kept on hand with enough powder and balls. Five Indians who went to get food were caught and publicly whipped. Soon after, an Indian was killed; then three white men were wounded and a white mail-carrier killed. The chief, Emaltha, who was friendly to the treaty, was assassinated. The war had begun.

It was now 1836 and Osceola was thirty years old. Hearing that Major Dade, with 110 officers and men, was to pass along the military road from Fort Brooke at Tampa

He drove his knife through and through the paper

Bay, Osceola sent Micanopy and Jumper with 800 of his warriors to wait in ambush for them. It was so well arranged that the whole command except three men were killed. These three men escaped to Tampa and told the terrible story. Osceola had himself remained with a small force near Fort King, for he wished to kill the Indian Agent, his long-time enemy. Lieutenant Smith and the agent were walking quietly toward the sutler's shop, a half mile from the stockade, when a number of Indians set upon them and both were killed. The agent was pierced by fourteen bullets and the lieutenant with five. The sutler and four others were killed, and the store and out-buildings burned. The fire gave the first alarm at the fort. In the meantime, Osceola's warriors under Micanopy and Jumper had been so prompt that the first battle was over before their leader joined them. Then the dreadful war went on.

Osceola met General Clinch with 1000 regular soldiers at the crossing of the Withlacoochee River. There were not a thousand Indians, but Osceola brought them into battle like an experienced general. His men followed his own brave example and fought with tiger-like ferocity. Osceola is said to have slain forty of our officers and men with his own hand. The Indians fought till their ammunition was gone, and then with bows and arrows and knives. After this, Osceola went through many battles, but he never despaired and never surrendered till the fearful battle came when the Indians were defeated by General Taylor. Then the waters ran with the blood of Uncle Sam's quarreling children and Osceola's men were scattered to the four winds. Even then Osceola would not have been captured but for an act of treachery. He was asked to come to a conference at a camp not far from St. Augustine. He came

16

with some of his warriors, trusting to the word of the commander, but he and his companions were at once surrounded and carried to St. Augustine as prisoners of war. Our officers said it was right to do this because Osceola had not kept his promises in peace or war, but we do not like to think that the officers and agents of Uncle Sam broke their word, even if an Indian chief did not keep his. Though Osceola fought in the Indian way, and hated the treatment that the white people gave the Indians, still, we know he did not hate the white women and children, and constantly told his warriors to treat women and children with kindness.

After he was taken to St. Augustine he was in a sad condition. His spirit was broken by defeat and imprisonment, and he grew feeble as he realized there was no escape. When he was taken to Fort Moultrie in Charleston Harbor he knew that he should never see his own land again. Then he refused food, would see no visitors, and died, broken-hearted, after a short illness, aged thirty-three. He was a brave enemy, and respected as he had been by the Indian nation, his manly nature was too proud to be long under the control of the white man.

II

BILLY BOWLEGS AND THE EVERGLADES OF FLORIDA

WATERVLIET ARSENAL, near Troy, N. Y., is one of the places where Uncle Sam keeps his guns and powder, and as I was an ordnance officer, that is, an officer whose duty it is especially to look after the things to shoot with, I was on duty at that post when word came to me from Washington that the Indian chief, Billy Bowlegs, had broken out from the Everglades of Florida to go on the war-path, and that Uncle Sam wanted me to stop looking after guns in Watervliet, and to look after them in the South. Little John McCarty, the son of our housekeeper, brought the news in a big envelop to the stone house where we lived, and alhtough it was not long before Christmas, 1856, I had to leave the family, including a little thick-necked, long-maned, hard-bitted Morgan pony, of which we all were very fond, for he had taken us up and down many a long hill. Saying good-by to my little boy, I told his mother, his grandmother, and my brother Charles to be sure and remind Santa Claus not to forget him on December 25th, and started for the South.

It took eight days by train to reach Savannah, Georgia, seven days by boat to Pilatka, and two days and nights in an old-fashioned stage-coach through palmetto roots and over sandy roads to Tampa Bay, Florida, where Fort Brooke, one of Uncle Sam's Army posts, was situated near the sea-shore. Here I was told that I must go farther, for General Harney was down the coast at Fort Meyers and he wanted to see me. Some soldiers rowed

"Billy Bowlegs"

me out to a steamer which was lazily swinging back and forth at anchor on the surface of the beautiful bay. It was freezing cold weather when I left Watervliet, but here the air was mild and pleasant, like our summer in the North. By the next morning the steamer was lying off the mouth of the broad Caloosahatchee River, which empties into the sea. The name of this river is half Indian and half Spanish. In English it means the Charles River, and its current is so strong that, although we had eight trained oarsmen to row us, yet it took nearly all day to go the twenty-five miles from the mouth of the river to Fort Meyers, where General Harney was staying. Fort Meyers, like many of Uncle Sam's forts, is an army post with no fortifications at all. The barracks where the soldiers lived, and the officers' houses, were built of logs, and so strong that it was thought they could be defended against all the Indians of Florida.

Here I met my general and learned something of the fierce Indian leader Billy Bowlegs, who kept a large part of Florida in a state of alarm for over a year.

You remember the old chief of the Seminole Indians, Micanopy, and how Osceola sent him to waylay and fight Major Dade and our soldiers in the first real battle of that Seminole War? Micanopy had with him at that time his young grandson, who was about twelve years of age. This boy rode a small Florida pony on that eventful day, and when the battle began he led his pony behind a clump of earth and grass, called a hummock, and stretching the lariat, a slender hair rope, on the ground, the pony understood that he was meant to stand still. Then the boy took his bow and, stringing an arrow ready for use, lay down in the tall, thick prairie-grass near Micanopy. I suppose this boy's real name was Micanopito—for that means the grandson of Micanopy in Spanish—but he began when he was so very young to ride astride big horses, and on top of such large bundles, that it made his legs crooked, and his father, who knew a very little Spanish, nicknamed him Piernas Corvas, meaning bowlegs. When he grew up, Natto Jo, a man who was part Indian and part negro, called him *Guillermito á las piernas corvas,* meaning to say little William Bowlegs; but when Natto Jo came into our camp, and spoke of him by that name, the soldiers asked what it meant and turned it for themselves into Billy Bowlegs.

This chief was thirty-two years old when he first led his warriors into battle. About 350 Seminoles refused to go West when most of the Creek Indians went to live in Indian Territory after Osceola died, and it was these who followed Billy Bowlegs. He was a full-blooded Seminole, a perfect marksman, and his powers of endurance were as remarkable as his ability to appear and disappear in the most unexpected manner. This was possible because he was so well acquainted with the Everglades, and never went very far from that region. The Everglades is the name given to a large, shallow lake in Florida about 160 miles long by sixty miles wide. It contains many islands, some large and some small, but all covered with trees. The whole is very marshy and full of the intertwined roots of tree-trunks. Long streamers of moss hang from the trees, and while the Indians in their light canoes could push among the vines and thickets so that no trace or sign of them could be seen by a white man, it was impossible for the soldiers to follow them on horseback or on foot, for the water was up to a man's waist. The Indians hid their women and children in these Everglades, and scouts sent to hunt found no trace of them during a search of weeks and even months.

As I listened to so much about Billy Bowlegs, I became very impatient to see him, and it seemed to me that the only thing which Uncle Sam could hope to do was to make peace with him and his warriors. The few Indians I saw seemed shabby enough in their tattered garments, for although each had been given a good blanket, they were untidy savages and always turned their eyes away. I asked sometimes, "Is Billy Bowlegs here?" But he was always somewhere else.

In this last Indian war in Florida, Bowlegs had more warriors than horses, but in spite of his short, crooked legs he could go on foot through weeds and swamps faster than any other Indian. Once he took about 100 of his men on foot from the Everglades sixty miles to Lake Kissimmee to attack one of Uncle Sam's stockades, which was in charge of Captain Clarke. This stockade was made of small logs planted close to each other, deep

27

in the ground, so as to form a fence. Square holes, or "loopholes," were left in this stockade so that the soldiers could push their rifles through.

Once in the early morning, while it was still dark, Captain Clarke thought he heard a noise outside of the stockade. He waked the soldiers at once, but although they looked very carefully, they could not see anybody outside and there was no more noise, but when the sun came up and it was light they saw the Indians all around. It was Billy Bowlegs and his followers. They gave a great warwhoop and rushed upon the stockade from every direction. The soldiers fired through the loopholes in the stockade and after a while the Indians, taking those who had been wounded with them, went about a mile away, where they hid in a large hummock. The soldiers followed and tried for a long time to drive the Indians from the hummock, but at

Billy Bowlegs and his retinue

The above group represents a party of Indians, as they appeared in New York, in 1840 — the famous "Billy Bowlegs," four other Indian chiefs, and an interpreter. Billy was a short, stoutly-built man of about forty years of age; and was clad in a calico frock, leggings, a belt or two, and a sort of short cloak. On his head he wore a kind of turban, inclosed in a broad silver band and surmounted by black ostrich feathers, by which he was distinguished from the other chiefs. Billy was the chief of the Seminoles, and nephew of the old chief who ruled the tribe at the commencement of the Seminole war in 1835.

last they gave it up and went back to the stockade. When General Harney heard of this he sent a hundred mounted soldiers to help those in the stockade, but by the time they arrived Billy Bowlegs and his warriors had left the hummock and were safe in the Everglades once more.

About this time General Harney left Florida and Uncle Sam sent Colonel Loomis to try and overcome Billy Bowlegs. The first thing this officer did was to send many companies of soldiers in different directions toward the Everglades. One party came upon some Indians moving from hummock to hummock. There were men, women and children, and Billy Bowlegs was leading them. The mounted soldiers rushed upon these Indians and fired, killing some and capturing others, but their leader, Billy Bowlegs, made his escape. When Colonel Loomis heard that some of the children had been wounded, he felt so badly that he made up his mind to try another way to overcome Billy Bowlegs. He sent for me and told me to go into the Indian country and try to have a talk with the chief. Two companies of soldiers went with me and also an Indian woman called Minnie, to guide us. She took her child along. Natto Jo, the half-breed, went too, to speak for us to the Indians in their own language.

Through forests and over prairie lands we went. One day, when we came to a beautiful open glade I rode with Lieutenant S. D. Lee some distance ahead of the main body of soldiers. As we were riding I turned to see the soldiers, but they were out of sight. I looked around to speak to my companion and to my astonishment saw the whole company, men, wagons, and horses, marching along in the sky above the horizon to my right. We hastened on expecting soon to come to them, but just as we supposed we had reached them they disappeared. Such a wonderful picture is called a mirage, but so real did it seem that we could hardly believe it was only a reflection of the company, which was still far behind. All the journey the Indian woman had been so dirty that we thought her most unpleasing and savage, but when we stopped near Lake Okechobee she began to sing cheerily. She washed her face and hands, combed her hair, and dressed herself and her child in respectable and clean clothing, which she had carried in a bundle,—adding many beads and some wild flowers. We could hardly believe her the same person, but when I spoke to Natto Jo of this wonderful change he said in his usual funny English: "He 'll fool you and Natto Jo mañana (to-morrow)."

But we had to trust her, so we sent her with messages to Billy Bowlegs and she promised to come back soon with an answer. For a few days we waited near the lake, but she never came and at last we went back as we had come. Yet I am sure that her visit did good and that she gave my messages to the chief, for while the Indians came out after this from the Everglades to seize supplies, as they could raise no grain during the war in their hiding-places and needed food, and while they attacked small numbers of our soldiers now and then, still, when Johnny Jumper, the son of Osceola's old lieutenant, finally came on a visit from the Indian Territory with some other Indians, he learned from a warrior who had been wounded and captured at Lake Kissimmee, that Billy Bowlegs would like to come and talk about peace, but he did not dare to do so. He was afraid that the white people would pay no attention to his flag of truce and might shoot him. Johnny Jumper was a friend to the white man, and when he heard this he took "Polly," a niece of Billy Bowlegs, with him and went straight into the

34

" The soldiers tried for a long time to drive the Indians from the hummock "

Everglades to see the chief. They succeeded, and the result was that Colonel Loomis sent out a proclamation, saying that the Florida war was ended, and Billy Bowlegs, with 165 other Indians, went with one of Uncle Sam's army officers to "The Indian Territory" to live. Nearly all the Indians that were left followed the next year.

Except for the chief, Sam Jones, who was too old to go, and a few of his followers, the Everglades was now empty; but Billy Bowlegs, firm and determined to the last, left his country and passed beyond the Mississippi to join his brother Seminoles in other lands. Yet his soul, undaunted, could not brook this change from the wild and free life of the Everglades, which he had always known, and in less than a year after his arrival in the new land he died, honored and praised, as always, by his own people.

37

III

THE Yuma Indians of Colorado live on the banks of the Colorado or Red River, which is very long and flows between high banks. In the Mohave country it passes through the Grand Canyon of the Colorado, a gorge quite as broad and as deep as the famous Yosemite Valley of California. After leaving the Grand Canyon, the red waters of the river flow through the most barren country of our land. Sometimes there is not one drop of rain for as much as three years, and the vast region is like the Desert of Sahara except right along the river banks.

38

The officers and soldiers at Uncle Sam's army post, which is called Fort Yuma, have made ditches from the river, and by watering the land it has become a real garden. They raise vegetables and have planted rows of trees which grow well, for the soil is rich when it is watered, but dry as a bone when left alone. There are wonderful magnolia trees here, high, with broad branches, the pure white blossoms looking like so many doves among the green leaves. The century plant and palmettos stand guard along the roadways within the stockade, and hedges of cacti form impassable barriers. Prickly pears and figs grow in abundance, and everything is green and beautiful, but only because here water has been brought to land which was once called the American desert.

The Indians knew long before Uncle Sam's soldiers came that water makes a wonderful difference in this country, so they clung to the river, never moving far away from its banks, and for this reason are called Yumas, meaning "Sons of the River."

When the tribe was large they cultivated the land along its banks, pine woods sheltered them, and they kept everything green while the river gave moisture to their land, so that things grew, which gave them food and support.

Later, the tribe became small because so many had been killed in battle; and then they were very, very poor. The men, it is true, needed little clothing, but what they had was in rags. They were tall, large, fine-looking men, but their hair was rough and coarse, unkempt, and falling loosely over their shoulders. Some of the girls were good-looking, wearing fresh cotton skirts and many strings of beads, silver ornaments and thin shawls which they drew over their faces as the Mexican women do when they are spoken to. They

pride themselves upon their fine beaded moccasins also.

I first saw these Indians when President
Grant sent me to see what could be done to
make them more comfortable. When I
reached Fort Yuma it was hard to believe
that the country was such a desert as I had
been told it was, for the fort was really
an oasis. On my way to the place where I
was to meet the Indians I passed through a
Yuma village and saw women trying to cook
over small sage-brush fires, using broken pots
and kettles for boiling some poor vegetables.
Children were playing on the high banks
which overhung the river. Some had bows
and arrows; some slings with which they
were shooting pebbles as far as they could
into the river below them. Their hair fell down
like a pony's mane, floating over their backs
and half covering their shoulders. They were
without clothing, but I heard their ringing

voices, and they seemed as happy as other children. When I left the village I went by boat to the camp of the chief. It was like a poor gipsy camp, an irregular bivouac under some scrubby trees. A great many Indians, both men and women, had rowed over with us to join the Council, and it was a strangely mixed assembly. They clapped their hands and gave an Indian whoop as Captain Wilkinson and I sat down upon three-legged stools, made of pieces of plank a foot square.

The chief, Pasqual, was about eighty years old. He was very tall and thin, his dirty, tattered cotton shirt was open in front, exposing the bones of his chest. He wore no leggins, but some old moccasins on his feet guarded them from the thorny bushes. His gray hair was put back from his high forehead and reached to his shoulders. He received us with the dignity of a king, holding himself as straight as an arrow without a bend in neck

Pasqual

or body, then sat upon a bench lower than ours. The interpreter, a merchant of the village, who had acted as Indian agent for Pasqual, knelt near me, and all the Indians clustered around, while a dozen or more Mexicans and Americans took positions where they could see and hear.

Perhaps because of my own rank and because I was a messenger from the President, this old chief seemed somewhat humbled as he sat upon that low rough bench and began the story of his life. He began, as Indians always do, with compliments, saying that it was kind of me to come and see such a poor Yuma chief, and that he heard very good things of President Grant, for the Indian agent said he was a true friend to his poor Indians.

"But I was not always poor," he said, and then went on with his story. He was born on the banks of the big, red river, but far from this place. When he became a young man he learned to shoot with a long, tough bow, and had plenty of arrows in his belt. His father was killed on the Gila in a battle with the Tontos, and he was made war chief and "head chief" of the Yumas in his place. At that time the Yumas held all the land from Colorado to the great sea west and on this side north to the great bend of the Colorado River. East, they reached as far as the Tonto-country.

Then the white people came and fought with the Mexicans under Santa Anna, the man with one leg, and took California and the Yuma country on both sides of the Colorado River. At this time the Yumas and the Mohaves were one nation. All planted fields together and had enough food, but some soldiers and "white teachers" quarreled with the Yuma Indians. Suddenly the Indians were surprised by white soldiers, who came upon them under a very fierce and terrible captain.[1]

Pasqual got his warriors together and fought very hard. They drove the white men back many times, but the great captain had great guns and powder and balls, and the Indians had only spears and bows and arrows.

Twenty-five years later I met this great captain of whom Pasqual spoke. He fought the Yuma nation and defeated them more than once in 1848. He told me that the right way to deal with the savage Indians was to fight them, fight them, fight them, till they gave up. Then they would always be good, peaceable Indians. He said that the Yuma Indians were often gigantic in size and could beat the soldiers skirmishing. They ran behind rocks, logs, or knolls, and sometimes even came out boldly to face the regulars, but

[1] Captain Heintzelman, later general in the Civil War.

they had only bows and arrows, knives and spears, while we had cannon and muskets. This may be one way to get the country, but I cannot think it the right or the best way. At any rate, Pasqual's warriors were killed and many more wounded and carried away prisoners by the great captain.

Then the young chief's heart was broken, and he gave up the fight. The captain talked well, but after this the Yuma Indians grew poorer -and poorer. Although they made ditches and tried to raise corn and vegetables and trade with soldiers, white men, and Mexicans, still they remained poor and sick.

Now, the *old* chief had come to implore help for his children. He begged me to ask the President to give money for a big ditch to bring water to make the poor land better, and for more good land for the Yumas. Then, if they would let the *bad* Mexicans and white men alone and work on their own land, he

48

Pasqual visits San Francisco

hoped the tribe would rise up again and be strong and happy.

The old chief was greatly loved by his people. I saw one little fellow about five years old run to him and look up in his face. The old Indian smiled upon the boy and ordered a woman near the shore to give him a piece of bread. The chief guessed the meaning of my questioning look and told me the little fellow's name, "Juanito."

FOURTEEN years after this Council, Pasqual came to see me in San Francisco. He was one of the oldest Indians I have ever seen, about ninety-four years of age, but, if anything, brighter than when I visited him in Arizona. With him came a young Indian who spoke English and acted as his aide and interpreter, and this Indian was the boy Juanito. The aged chief had taken this long journey to ask me once more to help his children, the Yuma

Indians. They did not want to be sent to live with the Mohave tribe, for these Indians, he said, did not like the Yumas and would not treat them well. After he had spoken for his people, who were always nearest his heart, he enjoyed looking at the new surroundings. Although he was nearly one hundred years old he had never seen a large city before. How happy and childlike he was about it all! To walk in the streets, leaning on the strong arm of Juanito, who was as curious and observing as he; to watch the crowds of people and the many new and strange things; but above all to ride up and down the hills on the cable-cars.

He stood straight and tall before me as he said good-by and started back by a coast steamer. Then he went up the Colorado in a smaller boat, finally landing in safety on the east bank of his beloved Red River.

Without Christian teaching, without reading a book, only once visiting a large town, this dignified hero studied the wants of his people, fought their battles, behaved nobly under defeat,´ and was too noble ever to be completely crushed, though he lived for many years in neglect and extreme poverty. May this great son of the river, Pasqual, find his reward in the better land.

IV

ANTONIO AND ANTONITO

THE Pima Indians, who live on the banks of the Gila River (pronounced in Spanish Heela), are the most civilized of any North-American Indians. They live in houses, manufacture useful articles, and are known for simplicity of character, peacefulness, and honesty. But they have had their wars. A battle took place near the "broad trail," which is now sometimes called the Temple Road. Ursuth was the chief then, and he led his people against a band of

Apache Indians. The Pimas were far out-numbered by Apache warriors, and yet many were killed on both sides, but, although Ur-suth received three wounds, he was able to keep the Apaches back till the Pima women and children had escaped and reached a place of safety.

The Apaches always began the wars, but the Pimas were never slow to follow and fight them; they gained the advantage sometimes by making night attacks. They would come upon the Apaches with clubs and knives, and kill them in their sleep. Then, like all Indi-ans, the Pimas would carry off as many cap-tives as they could secure. These they sold in Mexico for sixty to one hundred dollars apiece, being paid in clothes or live stock. After a battle they would have wonderful dances to celebrate a victory.

When Ursuth grew too old to lead the war-riors, Antonio took his place and became the war chief. Soon afterward there came a year when there was no food in all the Gila Valley, so the Pimas took their wives with them to the San Pedro River. Here they made a camp for the women, and the men mounted the few Indian ponies and rode off in search of food. When they returned the camp and all the women were gone, for the wild Apaches had stolen in and taken everything. This was a fearful return, but Antonio lost no time; he and his warriors did not rest till they had overtaken the robbers in the Sierra Mountains. Here they had a terrible battle, but the Pimas won, and rescued the women who had been taken captive.

Later Uncle Sam had a fort near where the Pima Indians lived, and he sent General Alexander, one of his officers, to take care of it.

After a while, in the year 1868, this officer was obliged to make war upon some Apaches, for they were stealing cattle and horses from the Pimas and white people. A hundred Pima Indians went with General Alexander and helped him make many charges over hills, rocks, and streams. Their wild ways and brilliant dresses delighted him during his great march into the mountains.

The Pimas are proud of the fact that they have never killed a white man. They hate the Apaches and make war against them, but have always been the white man's friend.

General Alexander and his wife were great friends of these Indians, but were sorry to see that they believed in many foolish things; Antonio as well as all the rest. They tried to cure sick people by rapping on rude drums or shaking rattles day and night beside them. Some of the chief men of the tribe taught the warriors to get drunk at their feasts, and to play games which made it possible for a few Indians to gain all the property of the tribe.

57

They did all sorts of silly things, too, in time of famine, to bring food. The General often talked to Antonio and told him that there were good white people who lived far away in the East and that some day they would send a good man to live among the Pimas. He would not want their land or their money, but would come because he loved the Indians and wanted to do them good. What he told them would be the truth, and Antonio could trust him when he came. The chief listened. He believed and waited for the great teacher to come.

Three years went by, then a German named Koch went to live in Arizona. He was a Christian missionary and he wanted to help the Indians. The Indian agent built a small school-house for him, and here he began to teach the Indian children. Louis, one of the boys, could speak Spanish, and with his help the children taught the Pima language to

Louis, the interpreter

their teacher. The German word Koch is the same as Cook in English, and Mr. Cook, as he was called, worked hard till he could speak Pima, while the Indian boys and girls learned to speak English, though so carefully did they follow their teacher that these children, born and brought up in America, spoke English with the same German accent that Mr. Cook had, though he was born far away in Germany.

After this good man had learned to speak the Indian language he talked to the older Indians. The chief had been waiting for the coming of just such a teacher and he listened to what he taught, and profited by it.

In 1872 some bad white men went to live on the banks of the Gila River, above where the Indians had their homes. They dug deep ditches and drew away a large part of the river. Of course, their fields and gardens were well watered in this way, but they cut off a great deal of water from the Indians, who depended upon water from the river to make things grow in that dry country, where hardly any rain falls. More than half the crops of grain and vegetables were lost in consequence, and the fruit-trees were nearly dead and could not bear fruit. Before these white men came the farms had been watered by ditches from the river which took water far up on to the land and then branched, so that water ran over each Indian's land and made the soil very rich. Some of the Indians were very angry and loudly complained, but these selfish white men only said: "The Pimas can not have the whole Gila; if we are above them that 's their bad luck." Some of the young Indians wanted to fight, and I was sent to see what I could do to arrange matters.

When I first saw him, the chief, Antonio, was a lame old man, of medium height, with a bright, intelligent face; his black hair, a little mixed with gray, hung in two short braids down his back. His forehead was clear and high, and his dark eyes, always gazing straight at you, were steady and searching. With him was his son, Antonito, about twenty-five years old. He was stouter than his father, and kept his eyes always on the ground until we were better acquainted, when he would look into my face.

We met in the office of the Indian agent, Mr. Stout; and Mr. Cook was there with Louis to help as interpreter. Mr. Cook told Antonio who I was. He said he would like to show me his house, so we walked three or four hundred steps to Antonio's house. It was like a big beehive outside, of rounded form and twenty or thirty feet across. The roof seemed to be made of hard clay such as is called by the Spanish word *adobe*. One side was square, and a door about four feet high and three feet across opened into it. As we entered after Antonio we stepped down two feet to the floor of hard sand and clay. On one side blankets were rolled up and placed against the wall. Saddles, guns, and belts hung opposite, and between were benches and some two or three Indian dogs. The Pimas have always lived in villages and built this kind of house, not as do other Indians, who live in tents. We talked a while but did not stay, for without any window or chimney the smell and smoke were too much for a white man to stand very long. On our way back to the office we often stopped to look about us and I saw that the Gila was a very strange river. It flows rapidly along on its way to the Colorado for some distance, then the water suddenly disappears and only a river bed filled with sand is seen, the surface of which is usually dry and white. A little farther on the water appears again. I thought at first there must be a channel beneath the sand and that the water followed on underneath, but our engineer told me that the sand, like a sponge, takes up the water of the Gila for a short distance in several places before it reaches the Colorado River.

After our first talk Antonio opened his heart to me. He told me that wicked men had led his young people away and taught them bad ways. He said his people had been on the war-path in the past, but that they loved best to cultivate the land, raise fruits, and be at peace. "Some of our young men," he said, "now want to fight these bad white men who steal our water. Louis and Antonito think that way, but Mr. Cook says 'no.' He is our teacher. The children have been to school to him and as soon as he knew our language he told them everything, about the President, the United States Government, and many other things. They have told me."

4   65

Some time after this, a hundred miles west of Antonio's village, I gathered part of five tribes of Apaches, two tribes of the Pueblos (those Indians who live in houses), many Mexicans, white citizens, and some American soldiers. This was to be a great peace meeting, and I wanted Antonio, who was my friend, to come and tell the other Indians about me. But he was too old and lame, so Mr. Cook and Louis came, and Antonio, the chief of the Pimas, sent his son, Antonito, to the council in his place. He said his son would soon have to speak everywhere for the tribe and "might as well begin now."

At the end of the council the old enemies, Apaches and Pimas, embraced each other, while tears of joy ran down their cheeks. One strong active warrior said to Louis: "Look on the man you killed in battle many suns ago." It was indeed an Indian Louis had left for dead on the battle-field, and seeing

66

"'Look on the man you killed in battle many suns ago'"

him he was greatly frightened, for he was very superstitious. But when he realized that this man was quite alive they embraced each other in promise of future good fellowship.

Later Antonito went with me to New York and Washington with a party of ten Arizona Indians, and the new and startling experiences did much to bind them forever to the interest of this great peace.

I made a second trip to Arizona later and on my way north visited the old Chief Antonio. Mr. Cook and Louis with Antonito had returned safely from the East, and Antonio never tired of hearing about the marvels they had seen and heard.

When I left with Antonio's consent and Antonito's encouragement, I took two Indian lads with me, intending to place them in school. At first they were pleased with the idea of going where Antonito had been, and of seeing the wonderful things he talked about, but when we reached a stage station beyond Marecopa Wells the boys were so frightened and homesick that they cried aloud. The interpreter could not quiet them, but a rough woman in the station, who had said she hated Indians and believed they should all be killed, was so very sorry for the boys that she began to cry too and begged me not to take the children away. I sent the lads back to Antonio by the interpreter, but a few years later Antonito brought these same boys with some others, including his own son, to the school at Hampton, Virginia, and stayed with them there for about a year, learning all that he could. He was very lonely so far away from his own people, and was delighted when he found out that my son, whom he had seen in Arizona, was on duty at Uncle Sam's great fortification called Fortress Monroe, which was less than ten miles from Hampton.

Often Antonito would walk all the way over and sit near Lieutenant Howard's quarters, waiting to catch a glimpse of him. He did not always speak, but took a good look and went away with a contented and satisfied expression on his face, just because he had seen this old friend.

Ursuth, very old, was still living when I first visited the Pimas. Antonio never learned to speak English, but learned something new every day, for Mr. Cook taught the children and they told him. Antonito saw much more of the world than the chiefs who went before him, but like them he loved those who were his friends, and the friends of his people, and was always true to them.

V

FAR away near the Aravipa River in Arizona, one of "Uncle Sam's" young officers rode at the head of a company of soldiers. They had marched eighteen miles already in a deep ravine, the bottom of which was filled with coarse sand. In the rainy season this ravine was filled with water, but now it was what the Mexicans call a "dry arroyo," for there had been no rain for many weeks. Just at the mouth of this arroyo was the Aravipa River, coursing serpent-like across their path. It was not very broad nor very deep, but they were glad to see even a little water.

72

The march had been a hard one. Every step in the sand was like walking in loose snow, and the mules which drew the baggage wagons were tired and did not want to go. At sight of the Aravipa River flowing along between bright green cottonwood trees, the mules began to bray loudly and to pull hard to get their noses into the stream. The soldiers broke ranks and ran up the river, each to get a good drink of clear water and fill his canteen. A short way beyond was a beautiful grassy meadow, and here the little company pitched their tents, naming their camp for the great leader who had become our President—Camp Grant.

Now, six miles away from the cottonwood trees where the soldiers crossed the Aravipa River there was a deep cut or canyon. It was steep and high and rocky on one side, but so sloping on the other as to make a nice, safe sleeping-place for a tribe of Indians. Here

73

were beautiful springs of fresh water; the air was warm and the Indians made warm houses for themselves. First, they dug hollow places in the ground, lined with soft leaves or deer skins, and then protected these hollows from the sun by bushes or leafy branches laid across scrub trees, which grew to a considerable size on the cross ridges running to the bottom of the canyon.

This tribe of Indians is called "Aravipa Apaches," and if the young officer had believed the reports he had read in the newspapers or heard from rough Mexicans he would have supposed them thieves and robbers. But he had not believed these stories, for he was a strong friend to the Indians, and when he was sent to protect the Indian Agent, who was afraid to live alone among them, so far from any soldiers, he made up his mind to find out what was the real truth. As soon as the camp was in order, he took a

Santos

guard of six men with him and went to an old frame building a quarter of a mile down the river. This was the Indian Agency. Of course, the Agent could not speak Apache, so he had a queer-looking little man, half Mexican, half Indian, to act as interpreter. This queer little man looked like a dark-skinned boy of twelve or thirteen, but had the husky voice of an old man, and was probably about twenty-five years old. He was called Concepçion.

When the young officer reached the Agency, instead of fearing to meet the Indians as the Agent had done, he told Concepçion to go into the canyon and ask the present chief of the Indians to come to the Agency for a talk. Concepçion said the old chief was Santos, but Eskiminzeen, his son-in-law, was the real chief. He would bring them both. True to his word, Concepçion returned with the two chiefs within two hours. Santos was a thick-set, short-necked man, not very tall, but with a finely shaped head. His straight black hair was parted in the middle and cropped all around, so that the ends just touched his shoulders. He wore a common waistcoat over a poor shirt, open at the throat. A strip of cotton was around his waist, like a short skirt, and he had low beaded moccasins on his feet. Two strings of bright beads hung around his neck. The young officer took quite a fancy to him at once, in spite of this queer costume, for his eyes were mild and dark and looked friendly.

Eskiminzeen, Santos's son-in-law, had his hair in two long braids and was fully dressed in skins. He wore rings in his ears and a string of silver coins and little shells around his neck. In his hand was a small shawl, which he sometimes wrapped like a turban round his head.

At first, the young officer tried to talk

through Concepçion to Eskiminzeen, but the chief was a stammerer and stuttered so badly that it was very hard to understand him, and at last Concepçion gave it up.

"Sir Lieutenant," he said, "Eskiminzeen no talk good, me no savey!" (I don't understand.)

"Try Santos," said the young officer.

The chief raised his eyes and gazed steadily at the lieutenant, while he answered questions which were given through the interpreter.

He said that for a long time *he* was head chief of the Indians who now lived in Aravipa Canyon. They planted lands then, loved peace, and did not go on the war-path. When Tontos or Sierra warriors came, they fought them and drove them off, but they loved peace and when the enemy was beaten planted corn and other things once more. Then they hunted for deer and other game,

79

stripped and dried the meat for food; gathered corn and did not go on the war-path. When Santos grew old he made this young Indian, Eskiminzeen, chief. It was he who brought Santos and the Aravipa Indians to this valley and to the canyon. Santos said it was a good place, a good house, and all the tribe had come. They had done no harm. Eskiminzeen never began a war, nor did he steal horses or cattle, or rob and kill white people. They intended to live quietly and happily, but one night the men had a big dance. They were so tired that they went to sleep where they had danced. The women and children went to sleep a short distance away from the men. While they were all asleep, before the sun was up, a big company of white men and Mexicans came up and fired their guns right at the women and children. Some were killed. Little boys and girls were hurt very badly, and a few of those that were hurt, with many more who were well, no matter how loud they cried, were seized by the white warriors and carried far away.

Eskiminzeen and the Indians did not fight; they knew it was no use, so they ran into the Aravipa Canyon, where the deep gulf and high rocks protected them, and the white men did not follow.

After the young officer had listened to Santos he began to see what bad stories had been told about these Indians, so he had all which Santos said written down and sent it to Washington. President Grant, you know, was always a great friend of the Indians, and when he read what Santos had said he sent me to Camp Grant to try to bring about a good peace between these Indians and the white people.

When I arrived so many more soldiers and officers had been sent to Camp Grant that houses had been built and it was quite a big army post. I first went to visit Chief Eskiminzeen and Santos with Concepçion. It was hard riding, and Concepçion went ahead of me, shouting: "All right, all right, bueno Generâle!"

Under the shady cottonwood trees, where the arroyo and the river cross each other, I met white men and Mexicans (who brought many of the children taken away in the one-sided battle) and many Indians. Santos became my devoted friend and helper. I told him that we had the same Great Father, so we must be brothers, and he took my hand and gave me his heart.

The great question was what to do with the captive children. The white people and Mexicans said it was much better for the children to stay with them in their Christian homes, but the Indians said: "They are our children and we love them and want them with us." After many councils, I told them that the question

The meeting of General Howard and Santos

must be settled by President Grant in Washington, and that in the meantime the children should stay at Camp Grant. Here the Indians could come and see them, and if the white people wanted to they might also visit and talk to them. This pleased everybody and all were satisfied. Santos took a small, hard stone and laid it before him on the level ground, saying: "As long as this stone shall last, there will be a good peace and no one will go on the war-path any more." Then the Indians, Mexicans, and white people embraced each other and there was great joy.

Santos always carried with him a small book which I had given him. Of course, he could not read a word of it, but he never lay down to sleep without putting it under his head.

He was the first Indian who agreed to go with me to Washington. At Santa Fé he was dressed like a white man, and from there we

85

traveled many miles. Santos was deeply interested in everything he saw. The White House and the President made his heart beat faster. He was more silent than General Grant himself, but with beaming face he gazed upon the great leader as long as he could, and carried back to Eskiminzeen and his Indians an impression which *he* only could tell them about.

We traveled back by train to Pueblo, in Colorado. Then by an old-fashioned four-horse stage-coach to Santa Fé, and by horseback to Camp Apache. Here I left him, and my son, Guy Howard, then but sixteen years old, took a guard of soldiers and escorted him over the rough mountain trail to Camp Grant.

As Santos and Concepçion slowly rode through the Aravipa Canyon they were met with a shrill cry of joy. The cry echoed and reëchoed from hilltop to hilltop for miles and miles, and must have reminded many of the time before when, hardly knowing what to expect, I entered the canyon and Concepçion, going before, cheered my heart with his high, shrill shout of "All right, all right, bueno Generâle!"

VI

YOU remember the great peace meeting
near Camp Grant, where the Indian
children were given back, and how old Santos
put the white stone down and said that as
long as it lasted there would be no war.
After this the Indians were very friendly to
the white man, and so it seemed a good time
for some of the Indian chiefs to go East and
visit the great Chief in Washington.

Just about one month after the great peace
meeting the young Pima chief, Antonito, his
friend Louis, who spoke some English, and

88

Mr. Cook, the good Indian teacher, joined old Santos of the Aravipa Apaches, who came with his interpreter, Concepçion, to meet them near the crossing of the Aravipa River. Then they all rode on horseback to a field just south of Camp Grant, and here I met them. Captain Wilkinson, my aide, was with me, and we had a mounted escort of a sergeant and six soldiers. We were to go one hundred miles over a very rough, steep mountain trail to Camp Apache near the eastern border of Arizona, but we could take no wagons, so all our luggage was on four strong pack-mules. When we started I rode a large gray horse named Frank. He looked very fine indeed, but one of the officers at Camp Grant told me to be careful and not trust too much to appearances, for Frank was not used to long journeys as the mules were, and he was likely to grow lame on the stony road, or fag out. I patted the beautiful creature and we started

89

off, but I had hardly ridden twenty miles before Frank, beautiful as he was, gave out entirely. He was too weak for me to ride him any further, so I left him with a soldier to be slowly led to the nearest army station, and was glad indeed to take the soldier's mule for the rest of the journey.

We camped two nights beside good water, and found plenty of wood near by, and on the third morning our queer-looking cavalcade rode out of the surrounding forest into a beautiful mountain glade. A small river tumbled over the rocks and then cut its way through a deep and peaceful channel. The dark green of spruce- and pine-trees was around us, making a delightful spot in the great wilderness, which, toward the north and east, seemed endless. Among these surroundings we found a regular frontier army post, large enough for six companies of soldiers and their officers. This was Camp

Pedro

Apache. You may be sure that we were warmly welcomed, and every one tried to make us comfortable. When we were rested Major Dallas, the commanding officer, told me about the Indian tribes here. There were three bands, all Apaches. The nearest band, about one thousand strong, was only a few miles to the east. Pedro was their chief. Eskeltesela was the chief of another band. He was old and easy-going, but a good soul. His people quarreled some with their neighbors, Major Dallas said, but on the whole gave little trouble. About twelve miles away to the south was still another band, eight hundred strong. This was under a chief whom the white men called "One-Eyed Miguel," because he had only one eye. These chiefs, the Major said, were formal and ceremonious, and had plenty of complaints to make, so I might expect to have a visit from them as soon as they knew I was at Camp Apache.

93

And it was not long before they came. Pedro looked like a spare-boned, hard-working Yankee farmer, and tried to dress like a white man, for he had one white man in his band. Eskeltesela was handsome, with fine features and large, clear eyes. He dressed like a Mexican. After he had paid the usual compliments, he told me that his children had tried always to do good, but they were often hungry and wanted bread and some meat.

Last came One-Eyed Miguel. He was the biggest chief of all, and indeed was worth seeing. He was very tall, his hair hanging loose, long, and unbraided. He seemed to be watching all the time with his one eye, and he was always smiling. Evidently, come what might, he intended to be agreeable. Concepçion interpreted and told me that Miguel was glad to see "Washington Big Chief"; did I know that the Sierra Apaches came to the good Major now for food, but

One-Eyed Miguel

they had been hungry so long that if you touched them their sharp bones hurt you. They had good corn on their farms, too, only it was not ripe yet. I listened to what Miguel had to say, and then I asked him if he would go East with me. He thought about it for some time and then said that he would go. At this time, as Miguel had told me, all the Indians came once in two weeks to Camp Apache for food, and when they came Miguel took me to see his family. His wife and children crowded around me and smilingly begged me to take good care of Miguel and bring him back safely, and his wife said to me: "Whisky bad for Miguel, no let him drink." It was a good suggestion, and I pledged all the Indians who went with me not to drink any liquor while they were gone. Indians are very careful always to keep a promise, and every one kept the pledge faithfully.

Eskeltesela's wife shed tears at the prospect of his going so far away, but old Santos told her I was a great chief and would bring Eskelt back safely, so she was comforted.

Pedro would not promise to go at first, but he brought the white man who lived with his band to see me. This man was well educated, but he suffered from a fearful disease, so he left his own people to live among the Indians, and carefully taught the tribe and Pedro many useful things. He could act as interpreter, and after we had spoken together he told Pedro to go to Washington with me, and quieted the family who were afraid, till they said: "Go with the Tatah (Father) and come again."

About noon on the day of departure we drew out of Camp Apache. There were eight Indian chiefs beside Louis, Concepçion, Captain Wilkinson, Mr. Cook, and myself, who, with the soldiers, made twenty-six in all. We

98

had two army wagons and one spring wagon, the latter driven by a man called Jeems. Nearly all of us rode horses or mules, but any one who was tired could ride in the spring wagon.

The first day we made ten miles in woods all the way over a good, level road, and at night camped by a stream where I saw plenty of nice dry wood. When we were settled I proposed to the chiefs that we have a good fire, and asked them to help me gather some wood. Then how Miguel laughed! He told Concepçion to tell me that no big chiefs hauled wood, and sat down, still smiling at what he thought a great joke. Then I told Concepçion to tell me that no big chiefs chief as he was, and, calling Captain Wilkinson, we began to draw the dry branches. Laughing all the time, Miguel told the other Indians to come and help. They helped us draw large branches for the fire and never again refused to work when it was necessary. The next day we traveled thirty miles and left the forest behind us, but at night our camp was beside some cottonwood trees. The Indians led us to a good spring and as the next day was Sunday I decided to spend it here. When Miguel heard this, he rode to me on his Indian pony, and laughing, said: "I go to my house." Louis told me that the chief wanted something, but added, as he saw him ride off across the broad prairie: "No more Miguel." Two days passed! On Tuesday when we had about given him up, I spied a single horseman loping along toward us from the northwest. It was Miguel! He had kept his word to the Tatah, and was ready to go on.

The next Sunday we encamped beside a small river, but the water was so mixed with clay and sand that we could not make it clear. The animals would not drink, and every one

"He turned a back somersault into the river"

begged to go a few miles further to the Rio Grande and cross to the town of Albuquerque. I was about to do this when Captain Wilkinson, who had been roaming about, found a spring of good, clear water, so we remained. It was here that Louis became very angry over something and Mr. Cook told him that he was no Christian. Louis felt so badly about this remark that he came to me and asked if he might go back home, but I explained to him that Mr. Cook only wanted to help him to act as a Christian, and he was happy again. After this I often rode beside Jeems in the spring wagon. He talked all the time, and his local knowledge of robberies and massacres was wonderful; but it was very sorrowful, for while he told me the most thrilling stories of highwaymen, all the tales were very sad. I never heard him tell one cheerful story. He would wait till we were passing some lonely place and then would tell the sorrowful story of a robbery which had taken place there, till I almost expected to see the robbers rush out. For this reason we called him "Dismal Jeems." He had a hard time with his mules, for he could not reach those ahead with his whip, and one of them, "Lucy," would sway back in the harness and refuse to pull, just as if she knew. I gathered a handful of pebbles and, whenever she lagged, tossed one and hit her on the back. Then she would start up and was as smart as the rest. I believe Lucy thought the driver did this, and made up her mind to have revenge.

When we reached the Rio Grande the water was high and rushed along. We pulled the raft ferry-boat a mile up the stream and loaded it so as to shoot across diagonally with the current to an island near the Albuquerque shore. All of us were aboard except Dismal Jeems and the Indians. Jeems

Eskeltesela

jumped on the raft and landed just about three feet behind Lucy's slender tail. Her time had come! Quick as a flash her small hind feet struck him in the chest and with such force that he turned a back somersault into the river and disappeared beneath the water. We caught him when he came to the surface and brought him aboard, but he was wet and groaning. I confess I was frightened myself, for the river was rushing along very rapidly, but the Indians could hardly contain themselves as they sat on the bank. They were doubling up and rolling on the ground with laughter, crying out: "Jondaisie no bueno,"—"That mule no good."

At Santa Fé we left our escort horses and wagons to the Indian Agent and garrison, and now, dressed in good civilian clothes, took the four-horse stage for Pueblo. On the way I happened to speak of the earth as round, and when the Indians heard me they begged that

107

I would not say so, for people would think I was troubled with bad spirits; no one with sense could think the earth was round. They hardly knew what to say when I told them I knew a white man once who sailed in a ship all the way around it. How surprised they were over all the new things they saw. I watched when they first saw a railway, a train of cars, a telegraph line, a tunnel or a bridge; sometimes they were breathless and full of fear, at other times they showed great joy.

Once Eskeltesela said to me: "You think Indians all bad; look in my eyes and see if you see any bad." And indeed I did not as I looked into his frank, open face and bright, clear eyes.

Miguel carefully counted all the mountain peaks as we traveled, that he might surely be able to find his way back, but as the train rushed on he became more and more discour- aged and at last he told me he had given it up. He had trusted me to come, and would trust me altogether now. In New York I bought Miguel a glass eye. It was so much like the other eye that it was hard to tell which was which. The doctor told him to take it out and wash it now and then, but Miguel said: "No, no. Whoever heard of a man taking out his eye." He was very proud of this new eye, and had Louis write and tell his people that when he came home he would have two eyes instead of one. In Philadelphia I took the Indians through the large prison, and they saw the warden shut all the cells and close the bolts from a central station. They went along the halls and looked through the gratings. At last Miguel took me aside and said: "Do you think there is one innocent man in here?"

"Why?" I asked.

"Because I was once in prison at Santa Fé for a whole year, and I had done no wrong.

109

If there is one man here who is innocent I want to speak to him.''

I told him that every man had had a fair trial, and then he was satisfied.

In Washington we went to see the home where children who are deaf and dumb are taught to read and write, and to speak. Here the Indians were very happy. Miguel began by making rabbits with his hands and was delighted when the children understood what he meant. One after another the chiefs began to tell stories in the sign language, and although they could not make the white man understand in English, they could, strange to say, tell wonderful stories of animals and forests, streams and prairies, to the deaf and dumb children.

Here in Washington these "American chiefs" saw the "Great American Chief," our President, and then we started back once more for the West. At Camp Apache all the

Indians gathered to greet Pedro, Eskeltesela, and One-Eyed Miguel, and to rejoice over their safe return. I never saw more signs of real joy as they flocked around them, but One-Eyed Miguel was One-Eyed Miguel no longer, and all were curious to catch a glimpse of this ever-smiling Indian chief who came back from the white man's country with a new eye.

VII

COCHISE, THE CHIRICAHUA APACHE CHIEF

ONCE upon a time, far away in New Mexico, an Indian tribe lived on a large stretch of land near a place called Tulerosa. They had not always lived there, but now the white men said they must stay there and nowhere else, for there was much land, many trees, and plenty of water. But the ground was really too poor for the Indians to plant, and they said the water made the children sick.

The chief of this tribe, the Mescalero Apaches, was Victoria, a good man who was troubled for his people. He knew they were

112

discontented and wanted to go on the war-path and that it was better for them to keep peace.

Now not far away from Tulerosa Uncle Sam had an army post where some soldiers lived who believed that the Indians had good reason to be unhappy. They thought about it awhile and then wrote down all they had heard the Indians say and sent it in a letter to President Grant at Washington. President Grant wanted everybody in the whole country to be happy, so he decided to send some one out to Tulerosa to see just what the matter was and what could be done.

I was very busy just then in Washington, but the President sent for me and told me not to wait a minute, but go right out to New Mexico and find out about things; so, of course, I went.

After I arrived the very first Indian I saw was the chief, Victoria. He had been trying

113

his best to keep peace but there were Indians on the war-path near by, who made it just as hard for him as they could, and among these Cochise, the chief of the Chiricahua Apaches, was the most warlike.

He had been fighting for many years, taking prisoners from the long wagon-trains that passed by, burning the wagons, and driving off the horses and mules quite like an old German robber baron. He lived in a stronghold, a great fortress among the rocks, 'way up in the Dragoon Mountains, and from here he attacked stages until none could go along the highways or on any road near where he lived.

He never took prisoners. No, indeed; he killed all the white people he came across, and had never spared one, except a man the Indians called Taglito, which means Red Beard. His real name was Jeffords, and he was a white guide. How he alone came to be spared

114

nobody knew. Of course, there could never be peace till Cochise agreed to it, so I told Victoria I had made up my mind to try and see this powerful warrior. Victoria was horrified. He seemed to think this out of the question, for no white man had ever seen Cochise and lived, except this same scout, Captain Jeffords. But where there 's a will there 's a way, and I did not give up, and kept at Victoria to help me.

At last he said there was one Indian who might help me. This was Chie, the son of Mangus Colorado (Red Sleeve), a brother of the warlike Cochise. Chie's father, Red Sleeve, was killed by the white men when Chie was a tiny boy, so I could not expect much help from him, but it was worth trying and Victoria brought him to see me. He was a fine-looking young Indian, dressed in deer skin from head to foot, but with no cap, for his own thick black hair was cap enough.

115

To my surprise I found him inclined to be friendly, and he spoke so much of Jeffords and the love of his Uncle Cochise for the scout, that I decided to see the famous Taglito. He was out just then acting as a guide to a troop of soldiers, but the next day would return, and then I could see him.

As soon as he arrived the commanding officer sent him to me, and when he entered my tent I did not wonder that he was called "Captain." He was very tall and fine looking, with clear blue eyes and a long bright red beard.

I said to him: "They tell me that you have really been up in the Dragoon Mountains in the stronghold of the famous Apache chief—Cochise?"

"Yes, sir," he replied, "I have! Some people doubt it, but I assure you I made the old chief a visit last year."

"You are the first man," I said, "who has

116

been able to get beyond his Indian spies. I want to go to see him; will you take me?"

Jeffords looked very steadily into my face with his fearless eyes and then he said: "Yes, General Howard, I will; but you must go without any soldiers."

"All right," I said, "get ready to start as soon as you can."

Now Jeffords never hurried, he went to work very quietly and soon had done what was necessary. The next day he had a talk with Victoria and Chie and then came to see me again. He told me the first thing to do was to go with a few chosen Indians right out of our way back to the Rio Grande River. This seemed very funny to me, but Jeffords said that Victoria wanted very much to show General Howard his beloved country, Canyada Alamosa, and it would not do to disappoint him, for we needed his help very much and must keep him in good humor. Chie

117

promised to go with us to see his Uncle Cochise if I would give him a horse, and his wife, who stayed behind, a horse too. Again I said: "All right."

Jeffords thought that we could find Ponce, a friend of Cochise, not far from Canyada Alamosa, with his band of Indians. He was a wild fellow, but he could interpret from Spanish into Apache to perfection, and, besides, Cochise always believed what he said.

The next morning Victoria was ready to lead us with a small band of his men over the one hundred miles to the Rio Grande. Here he showed me the *Canyada Alamosa* and the *ojo caliente* (hot spring), where his tribe used to live. How they loved their old home! Would I not beg Uncle Sam to let them come back from Tulerosa and live once more in their own home land? Indeed, I was glad to promise to do what I could, and then I said good-by to the chief and his Indians. We must find Ponce. Jeffords and I were some distance ahead of our few followers when we came to the edge of an immense ravine. The Rio Negro (or Black River, because the water is so dark) flowed at the bottom. Along the banks of this river the farmers had planted corn and about three miles away we could see Ponce and his band helping themselves freely to the ripe ears. We rode as fast as we could till we were right in the midst of the Indians and then Jeffords, seeing that several were sitting in a circle playing games, sat down among them. I found some small boys a few steps away and began to amuse them, while the women watched with their eyes cast down as they worked over their pots and kettles or roasted the ears of green corn. By and by we told Ponce what we wanted and asked him to go with us as a guide and interpreter. He agreed to go if we would arrange to let his people meanwhile camp near a country store and be supplied from the store with food. Ponce was given a good horse, but he gave it to his wife and came to me for another. Now I had no more horses, so I told him he would have to ride behind on my horse. Sometimes I said he could ride, sometimes I would. With this arrangement he was perfectly satisfied, and, a party of nine men, we started for the border of Arizona, nearly 300 miles away. Ponce was a fat, good-natured, lawless fellow, lazy in camp, but capable of great endurance, of intense energy on the hunt for game and tireless when on the march. One day Ponce and I were riding quietly, his arms around me from behind, when he saw a deer track. At once he was alert, threw himself to the ground and, rifle in hand, pressed the deer till he had him caught in a thicket. I heard just one shot and then Ponce came back to the road with the deer swung over his shoulders.

We came, after a while, to a place called Silver City. It was only a little town, but there was a hotel where we could spend the night. After we had settled down some one told me that the people who lived in Silver City did not like Indians, and that they were going to take Ponce and Chie in the morning and kill them. When I knew this was true I told nobody but very early in the morning we all got up and were far away from Silver City long before the people who lived there were awake. Now there was one white man who hated Indians more than any one else in Silver City because some bad Indians had killed his brother. Well, he said that he would never be happy till he had killed an Apache, so he managed to get in front of us on the road. He was very angry when he saw us, and pulled out his gun ready to fire at Ponce and Chie. We were all on horseback, and when this bad man rode forward,

pointing his gun at the Indians, I believe I
was angry too. Anyway, I turned my horse
so that I was between the gun and our Apache
guides.

"Man," I said, "shoot them, if you please,
but you 'll have to shoot me first." This
made him more angry than ever, but I think
he must have been a coward at heart, after
all, for he did not quite dare to shoot the representative of President Grant, and so he
turned his horse and rode away; but Ponce
and Chie never forgot.

At last we reached the Mogollon mountain
range. Here Chie ran ahead of us and
started nine fires, far enough apart so that
anybody up in the wooded heights could see
the smoke and count them. It meant that we
came in peace and that there were nine of us.
After a little while Chie began to bark like a
coyote, and, as we listened a coyote bark
came back from the hills. Chie waited not a

"He did not quite dare to shoot the representative of President Grant"

moment, but ran quickly up the steep mountain side and disappeared among the trees. There was nothing for us to do but to wait for him to come back, and when he finally did return a small party of Cochise's Indians were with him. We had run into a small party of Cochise's Indians under Nazee, a sub-chief. The springs of water had dried up in the Chiricahua Range of mountains and that was why they were so far away. There was only one spring of water and that night we all shared it. In the morning with Ponce to talk for us we had a council with Nazee. He told us that we were still a hundred miles from Cochise, and that we would never find him as long as there were so many of us. Nine had not seemed very much to me, but I was determined to see Cochise, if I possibly could, and I sent every one back except Captain Sladen (my aide), Jeffords, and the two Indian guides, Ponce and Chie; so we started

125

once more. The next night we came to Rodger's Ranch, near Sulphur Springs, and Ponce and Chie were afraid of old Rodger's dogs, for he taught them to bark at Indians and bite them.

I had settled down for the night with a bear skin thrown over me and I told Ponce to stay by Captain Sladen, and Chie to come and sleep with me. Chie came to my bed on the ground, but when he had one look at my bear skin, he cried: "Shosh! Shosh! no bueno!" (bear, bear, no good) and refused to come nearer. I threw aside my bear skin and with two good blankets made him comfortable all the night, for afraid as he was of the savage dogs, he feared the bear skin more.

By the next day we were on the west side of the Dragoon Mountains. Here we rested by a clear flowing stream, while Chie went ahead of us into Cochise's stronghold. He did not return, but after awhile two Indian

COCHISE, THE APACHE CHIEF

lads rode toward us on an Indian pony. We received them as guides and offered them food and drink, which they seemed to enjoy. Then they were ready and pushed us on, riding behind us for five or six miles along a narrow ravine which led us finally into the very stronghold of Cochise. Forty acres were inclosed by a natural wall of rock, nearly a hundred feet high, and the only way in or out was by following the tiny mountain brook at the bottom of the ravine. When we were once in, it was very beautiful, for the grass was high, making a thick green carpet, and there were lovely shrubs.

Here we met another sub-chief, Nasakee, but there were no other warriors, only a few old men and many women and children. When we finally arrived at the stronghold, Cochise was off hunting, or hiding, and Nasakee said he could not tell us what Cochise would do with us when he came back, whether

127

it would be peace or war. I could see that
Chie felt very much afraid, for his uncle
might be angry at him for bringing us.
Ponce lost his usual jolly looks. Would the
great chief accept our peace message in the
morning, or would he kill us as he had killed
all the other white prisoners.

Whatever happened in the morning we
were safe for one night, and must make the
best of it. I wanted to talk with the boys and
girls, so I took out my memorandum book
and holding up an arrow, said: "What 's
that?" All the children cried: "What 's
that?" But I said: "Apache." One boy
saw in a minute what I wanted, and called
out: "Kah," so I wrote it down in my book.
Next I held up a bow. "Eltien," said the
children, and in a few minutes they were
bringing all sorts of things and telling me
their names in Apache. The women stood
around laughing, and so I spent the hours till
128

it was dark, and they went away to sleep under the trees, but when I put my head on a saddle and drew a blanket over me for the night, the children put their little heads all around on my cover and fell asleep, too. "Sladen," I said, "this does not mean war"; and very soon I fell asleep and did not wake till morning.

We had just had our breakfast when the chief rode in. He wore a single robe of stout cotton cloth and a Mexican sombrero on his head with eagle feathers on it. With him were his sister and his wife, Natchee, his son, about fourteen years old, and Juan, his brother, beside other Indians. When he saw us he sprang from his horse and threw his arms about Jeffords and embraced him twice, first on one side, then on the other. When Jeffords told him who I was, he turned to me in a gentlemanly way, holding out his hand, and saying: "Buenos dias, señor"

(Good day, sir). He greeted us all pleasantly and asked us to go to the council ground where the chief Indians had already gathered. Just as we started, Ponce told an Indian woman of the death of one of her friends among the Mescaleros. She listened for a moment, then gave forth a shrill, sorrowful, prolonged cry. Instantly every Indian stood still and showed silent respect till her repeated wailings had ceased. Then we went on and took our seats on the blankets spread for us and the council opened.

Ponce and Chie first told Cochise all about me, who I was, and what I had done for other Indians. He seemed very pleased with the story, and you may be sure we watched very carefully to see how he took it. Then he turned to Jeffords, and, calling him Taglito, told him to ask me what I came to him for. I answered him plainly that the President had sent me to make peace with him. He replied: "Nobody wants peace more than I do. I have killed ten white men for every Indian I have lost, but still the white men are no less, and my tribe keeps growing smaller and smaller, till it will disappear from the face of the earth if we do not have a good peace soon." He told me too how the war with the white men began. An officer had lost some horses, so he seized Cochise, his brother, Mangus Colorado, and some other Indians, and put them in a tent under guard. Cochise slit the tent with a knife and escaped. Then he seized the first white man he met and sent word to the officer that he would tie a rope round the white man's neck, hitch him to a pony and drag him along till he died. He would let the officer know that if he hurt Indian prisoners Cochise would drag white men by ropes till they died. But the officer would not hear. He took the Indians and hanged them all in Apache Pass. So war began, and

how could it be stopped? It was a dreadful
story. I had heard part of it before, but now
as I listened I was very, very sorry. Cochise
asked me how long I would stay. He said it
would take ten days for all of his captains to
come into camp, for they were off in all directions. I told him I would stay as long as it
took to make peace. Cochise was very much
afraid if any of his captains met the soldiers,
that the soldiers would fire on them and then
there would be war again, so I proposed to
send Captain Sladen to Fort Bowie, where
he could telegraph to all the soldiers in New
Mexico and Arizona not to fire on Indians,
but Cochise shook his head. "No, no," he
said, "you go. Leave Captain Sladen here;
we will take good care of him." I was very
willing to go, and felt sure that Captain Sladen would be safe even in Cochise's stronghold; but who would be my guide? All the
Indians were afraid, for I was going straight

132

among soldiers and they knew that most soldiers did not like Indians. Every one who was asked to be my guide, refused, even Ponce. At last Chie said he would go. I had saved his life once and he did not believe I would let the soldiers hurt him.

On two good mules Chie and I made the journey to Fort Bowie, and were back again by the second day, followed by a wagon with provisions, and a spring wagon drawn by four mules. While we were gone Cochise had chosen a new camp ground looking west. On a high rock, a quarter of a mile away, a large white flag on a pole stood out plainly. When we arrived we spread a piece of canvas on the ground and called it a table. I took the head and Sladen at the foot was carver. Cochise sat at my right and Jeffords with Chie on the left, Ponce and one or two others between. Here we ate three times a day, and Cochise and I became close friends while we waited for his captains to arrive. When they did come he held a Spirit meeting, taking his stand in a cozy place surrounded by small trees and wild vines. The women formed a large circle sitting side by side. The men inside the ring sat or knelt. Then followed a wonderful song in which all joined. It began like the growl of a bear and rising little by little to a high pitch, lasted ten or more minutes and then suddenly stopped. After this Cochise interpreted to the people the will of the Spirits, saying: "The Spirits have decided that Indians and white men shall eat bread together."

Then what a rejoicing there was. The Indian captains crowded around us and tried in every way to make me understand their joy, promising to keep the peace.

The next day we all went ten or twelve miles to Dragoon Springs, where we met Major Sam Sumner and the officers from

Fort Bowie who came at my request to confirm the "Great Peace."

When Cochise saw their uniforms in the distance he put his warriors at once into a sort of skirmish order, so that they could go forward for battle, seek cover, or run back in retreat at his word of command, but Captain Sladen and I brought about a happy and cheerful meeting, and the great good peace which we had made in the mountains was witnessed and confirmed. Then we went with Cochise and his five hundred Indians to Sulphur Springs near Rodger's Ranch. Captain Jeffords was made Indian Agent, and a large reserve of good public land was put aside for these Indians.

At last, when I was about to go, Cochise wrapped me in his arms and begged me to stay with him, but I said: "Your men obey you and I must obey the President, who wants me to come back to Washington and

135

tell him all about this 'Good Peace.' " And as I started for my home so far away I felt very happy, for I knew that while Cochise was a wild, desperate warrior, still his heart was warm toward me, and he was true to his friends and every inch a man "for a' that."

VIII

MANUELITO: A NAVAJO WAR CHIEF

YOU all remember how the Indian chiefs went with me to see the great American chief, President Grant, in Washington, and what a long ride we had before we took a train. Well, during that trip we rested for two days at Fort Wingate in New Mexico, and here for the first time I saw some Navajo Indians. They are cousins of the Apaches, and the language of the two tribes is so much alike that they can easily understand each other. Some people have said that the word Navajo comes from the Spanish word for knife, but probably it is an Indian word mean-

137

ing "well-planted fields." There were about 7000 in the tribe and they lived in log huts and raised corn, but their chief living was from large flocks of sheep and goats. From these they got plenty of wool which they dyed in soft colors and from which the women made splendid blankets known the world over for their beauty. These are the famous Navajo blankets you have heard about.

Now the Apaches and Navajos are cousins, but they have not always been friendly cousins, and just about this time they had been fighting each other rather hard. I am sorry to say that some of the white people thought it was a good thing for Indians to fight each other; it would help kill them off, they said. Of course it was a good thing for Indians to stop fighting white men, but the more they fought Indians the better. Now I thought this was all wrong, so I made up my mind to help the Indians to make peace with the Indians as well as with us. I had talked with my four Apache chiefs about this, and Santos was heart and soul with me. Pedro agreed with us, but Eskeltesela was doubtful, and Miguel made many objections. He said the Navajos had behaved badly to his Indians, had broken up their lodges and stolen their corn, and must be punished. Miguel had a good deal of the old war spirit left in him.

Well, here we were at Fort Wingate in New Mexico within ten miles of the principal Navajo village, and were resting for the night. We had taken the packs from our tired mules and let them loose to roll in the dust or run to the neighboring stream for water. We had unsaddled the horses and tied them near by. Our driver, Dismal Jeems, was getting supper and looked as happy as I ever saw him as he thought of the good things which would soon be ready. Then of a sudden we heard a loud whoop, as loud and long as any you ever heard in Buffalo Bill's show. One-Eyed Miguel was quickest to catch the sound and he knew what it meant. "Indian horsemen!" he cried, and sure enough there they were. Navajos in full gala costume; the men with bright blankets, streaming hair, and feathered hats, the horses with braided manes tied with red and yellow. To see them charging toward us was enough to make our hearts beat very fast, but the Indians only laughed and said: "Good, good! it is only a Navajo visit!"

The brilliant Navajos rode up at a trot, halted all together and came to the ground at once, each holding his bridle and resting his right hand upon the pommel of his saddle. The leader's horse stood waiting while he came toward me and stretched out his right hand, saying: "Buenos dias" (Good day).

This was Manuelito, the Navajo war chief. He was over six feet tall and weighed per-

"To see them charging toward us was enough to make our hearts beat fast!"

haps two hundred pounds. He was dressed all in deerskin with fringes on his coat and trousers and had on new leggings, buttoned at the side, and moccasins on his small feet. His hair was worn in many short braids and he had on a Mexican hat with a feather tucked into the brim and tassels hanging over. He wore many strings of beads around his neck, too, and was as fine a looking fellow as you ever saw.

Mr. Cook and Louis hastened to help Dismal Jeems, and we brought fresh stores from our packs and added a piece of canvas to our table-cloth. Then we sat down to supper and Manuelito was given the seat of honor at my right.

I think Miguel was not quite pleased at this, for he looked at me with a sly twinkle in his one eye and said, ''Bad Manuelito, he has not been war chief of the Navajos very long.''

After the supper Manuelito shook hands

again, said good night, and then they all
mounted and were off, but not before we had
planned for a council the following day at the
Navajo village.

The next morning the sun rose clear and
bright, and peace seemed to be in all that
beautiful land. By eight o'clock we were in
motion, but the Indians were thoughtful and
in no haste to lead the way. It took us two
hours to ride the ten miles. Some Navajo
scouts met us half-way and guided us to a
good spring. Here was a pretty grassy knoll
and we camped beneath a group of pine-trees
whispering in the summer breeze.

The principal chief, Juanito, was an old
man, lame and feeble. He limped over to pay
his respects to me, but pretended not to see
my Apache Indians. I asked him to be present at the council, but he whispered something
about my having the wicked Miguel with me,
and would not promise.

Everything was ready at the hour appointed for the council and I went to a small grove where a platform had been made of rough boards large enough for the Indian chiefs and myself. Mr. Cook, Louis, and Captain Wilkinson were with me, but the Indians did not appear. We waited and waited, till at last I remembered that neither party wanted to be first at the council. Then I asked Captain Wilkinson to go to Juanito and ask him to come and see *me* and bring his war chief with him.

Mr. Cook went to Miguel and told him I wanted to see him and the other chiefs, and Louis took my message to Santos. To be sure they all knew what it meant, and they came, watching each other carefully so that they should all arrive at the same moment. Miguel and Manuelito were both laughing when they stepped on the platform and soon all were talking cheerfully to each other. Santos took

145

great pains to make friends with Juanito and I began to feel sure of a good peace.

All Indian councils are very ceremonious— if you know what that big word means—and every one puts on his very best manners for the occasion.

Mr. Cook opened the meeting with prayer. I explained that the great chief at Washington had sent me on a peace mission and then Juanito said he always wanted peace, for he planted fields, raised sheep, ponies, and cows, and made blankets and many other things. His young men hunted in the mountains too, but the Apaches made wars.

Then Manuelito—splendid fellow that he was—stood up and spoke, for he was the war chief. He said he was all for peace. Of course he had had to fight the Apaches, Miguel knew that, but now he wanted a solid peace and to be friends with Apaches and all the Indians of New Mexico and Arizona.

146

Santos spoke in the same spirit and so did Miguel and the others.

After all had spoken Manuelito rose and asked to speak again. He had been thinking, and he said he was sure that he could stop all the badly disposed Navajos from hurting Indians or white men. He asked me to appoint twenty Navajo policemen and dress them in United States uniform, for then every Indian would know them and every white man would respect them. He asked me to give them the same pay as soldiers and then they would be proud and obey their leader and there would be no more trouble from the Navajos. This I agreed to do and Manuelito chose and commanded a fine body of Indians. So ended the council, but a month later on our return from Washington, we reached that same old Fort Wingate just before sundown and were met by Manuelito and his special policemen. They wore soldiers' hats with grand army cords and tassels, blue blouses and belts with two pistols to show their authority.

"Buenos dias, signor! Bueno — bueno," cried Manuelito, as he sprang to the ground and with bridle in hand stood ready to embrace me. Nearby the Navajos had a bivouac, and that night we camped near them. In the morning Manuelito rode beside me and told me that peace had prevailed.

When, after riding ten miles, we reached a beautiful spring we lunched together beneath some shady cottonwood trees and then Manuelito bade us farewell. As he and his men rode away my eyes followed this splendid leader, and I rejoiced that so fine a man was using every energy to bring joy and happiness to all about him—a war chief no longer, but a man of peace.

IX

CAPTAIN JACK, CHIEF OF THE MODOC INDIANS

IT was a queer country where the Modocs lived. Their land stretched along for sixty-five miles, measured on the straight line that separates Oregon from California, and it was thirty miles wide, some in Oregon and some in California.

Parts were fairly good for cattle and horses where the earth was rich, but most of it was in hillocks and knolls all stony and so much alike that it was not much easier, than on the water, to find the way without a compass. This land was called the "lava bed country," and it was well named. I suppose many thousands of years ago some volcano must have covered the ground with the volcanic stones and lava which left it so rough and bare.

Lost River, which is from thirty to one hundred yards wide, flows in and out among the lava beds till it joins the Klamath River and flows with it to the great Pacific Ocean. The banks of the Lost River are of great shelving rocks rising a hundred feet in air and beneath which are immense caves with openings leading to each other. In some parts there are a few small trees but no large timber, and to our way of thinking it is a desolate country indeed, but the Modocs liked it, especially the clear lake, Lost River, and bushy parts where quail, partridge, and wild turkey were found, for these Indians did not like to raise corn as white men do. They dug up wild onions, lily bulbs, and camas plants to eat, and found plenty of wild duck in the clear lake and Tule pond.

Captain Jack and his companions

In the year 1850 there was a general Indian war in Oregon and northern California. The white settlers, tradesmen, mechanics, farmers, and hunters, and rough men of the frontier, all came together led by a wild fellow called Ben Wright. Now Wright was not a good man, and he planned a surprise and made a dreadful attack upon forty-six Modoc Indians who were quietly sleeping in their tepees. But five of the Indians got away, and among them was one called Sconchin. He was only seven years old then, and almost all his father's family were killed.

This boy grew up to hate the white people. He was a tall, handsome Indian and belonged to a band of four hundred Modocs. Their chief was called Captain Jack by the white people, though his real name was Modicus. This chief was dark and brawny, and when he said a thing he would not change his mind. He called his tribe by their true Indian name,

Maklaks (the people), and wanted to be known by all white men and Indians far and near as "The very great all-time Chieftain." But he and Sconchin did not always agree, for Sconchin wanted to be war chief and make war against the white people all the time, while Captain Jack liked peace best, though he kept a war-bonnet on hand to use if he needed it. A war-bonnet, as you know, is like a winter cap of red flannel worn well back on the head with a mass of eagle and hawk feathers strung together and hanging down the back to the waist. This is only for war times, and Captain Jack kept one ready, but usually he wore an old soft gray hat with a cord round it, tassels peeping over the brim, and a single eagle feather to show he was chief. He always carried a rifle and two pistols tucked in his belt, but he thought peace with the white men was best for him and for his people. He was a very strong man, too, but he could not govern his Indians unless he did about what Sconchin wanted him to do.

In the year 1866 Mr. Meacham, superintendent of Indians for Oregon, sent word north and south to all the Indians to come to Fort Klamath and have a great talk. A good many Indians came and Mr. Meacham thought they really represented their tribes, but neither Captain Jack nor Sconchin were there. However, there was a great bargain, and the Indians agreed to take a small sum of money and go and live on the Klamath reservation. The Klamath reservation where they were to go is a lovely mountain country, only so far above the ocean that very little will grow in it. The lake near by is clear and delightful, with an island in the middle that looks like an ocean steamer, and the springs are cool and fresh. This was just such a place as white people like to go to in the summer, but for Indians no place at all.

155

Captain Jack said: "I have n't sold our land on Lost River and I won't leave it"; and Sconchin said: "Let us fight forever." But after a while, in 1869, Captain Jack said: "It is better than war." So with three hundred men, women, and children they moved the fifty miles up to the great Klamath reservation. But here something unexpected happened. The Klamath Indians were many more than the Modocs, and they were angry that the Modocs had come. The women and children quarreled and the Klamaths sent word to the agent that the Modocs were getting ready to go on the war-path. Then the agent moved the Modocs two miles away, but they had hardly put up their tepees when the Klamaths, Snakes, and other Oregon Indians began to bother them again.

At last Captain Jack, to avoid open war, one night with all his people fled back to their old home. But here they were not welcome, for the white settlers had their land and did not want them around. Of course, some white people were kind and knew the Indians told the truth when they said: "We have never lost our land, we cannot live in Oregon, we cannot hunt or fish on the reservation, nor gather lily bulbs, wild onions, or camas roots."

Good Mr. Meacham finally agreed to give them a reservation on the Lost River and Captain Jack said: "We will bargain and keep the peace." But at Washington people were busy doing other things, and for a long time no word came to say Mr. Meacham could give this land to the Modocs. Captain Jack's heart was sick and Sconchin said: "Mr. Meacham is like all white men, double-tongued and does not tell the truth."

At last a new Indian agent was sent to take Mr. Meacham's place. He believed the white settlers who told him that the Indians were bad and that they must be forced back to the Klamath reservation. So a company of soldiers under Captain Jackson went to make them go. The Indians were living in rough tepees or wigwams made of poles covered with brushwood. Some were on the river bank, some on an island. Captain Jackson and Captain Jack had a talk. The Indians did not want to go, but their chief said he would rather go than have war. Captain Jackson was trying, through the half-breed interpreter, to arrange the homeward march, when Scar-Faced Charlie, one of Sconchin's friends, angry and armed with a pistol, came out of his tepee. Captain Jackson ordered his immediate arrest by a sergeant, who also had a pistol. The soldier and the Indian fired at the same instant; then other soldiers and Indians fired. At the same time some white men, back on the island, were shooting into the Indian tepees. Five soldiers were killed or wounded and as many Indians fell. Then the Indians, in the confusion, got away. They caught up everything and ran southward, while Captain Jackson, gathering up his dead and wounded, made his way sorrowfully and slowly back to Fort Klamath.

The young Indians in their flight went through a white settlement and killed eleven white men and boys who came in their way, but they spared all the women and the smaller children.

You remember I told you of the wonderful caves on the banks of Lost River. To one of these Captain Jack led his band. From here he could see everything for five miles, and this cave led to other caves, so that without being seen he could make his way to the water's edge. Captain Jack had not more than seventy warriors, but they were in that strong place with food enough for three months for his men and for all of his women and children who were in there. Every Indian had a rifle and pistols and considerable ammunition. Against them Colonel Frank Wheaton of the army led six hundred soldiers. They were confident and ran briskly toward the stronghold, but the Indians were ready and beat back all the six hundred, having slain thirty-five of Wheaton's men and wounded many more. Colonel Wheaton was astounded. He drew off his soldiers and retreated twenty miles. A little later, however, the soldiers returned, bringing cannon and mortars. The mortars would throw a loaded shell high in air and drop it down in Captain Jack's fortress; lodging in the cracks and fissures, the fuse would keep burning till the shell, like that in blasting rocks, would explode and the fragments of iron fly in every direction. The Indians at first feared those "guns that fired twice every time," but soon they learned how to protect themselves.

"The soldier and the Indian fired at the same instant"

Then General Canby and Colonel Wheaton encamped before the cave with an army of soldiers. Rev. Mr. Thomas, Mr. Meacham, and some other peace-loving friends tried to bring about a good peace. They sent into the stronghold a half-breed interpreter and a conference was secured. Captain Jack even yet desired a peaceable settlement, but he did not like the offers made him of a new reserve near Lost River by and by after purchases of land could be made, and meanwhile for the Modocs to go down to Angel Island, near San Francisco, and be provided for. Though Captain Jack appeared to favor this arrangement the most of his warriors showed an ugly disposition, and, stirred up by Sconchin, were for *war, war!* Then Captain Jack, who had been planning in his mind a great blow, sent word that he and a few of his principal men, five in all, would meet General Canby and five of his peace men at a place between the lines about

163

a mile from the soldiers' camp. At the time appointed they met, but the Indians had pistols hidden in their clothing, and after a short talk, when everything was arranged, Captain Jack cried out: "All ready," and they fired.

The good general and Dr. Thomas fell instantly, and Mr. Meacham was badly wounded, but the others escaped, and Captain Jack's warriors drove back all the soldiers who were near enough for them to reach with their rifles; then they ran quickly back to their stronghold.

Now more troops came, and little by little Captain Jack saw his Indians grow less. The soldiers captured his spring of water and cut his people off from the lake till, in desperation, one night the Modocs without any warning fled to another cave, four miles away.

Some Warm Spring Indians, friendly to the white people, trailed the fleeing Modocs, and after many days and great losses among the soldiers the desperate Modocs had so few war-riors left and were so much in want of food and water that a part of them came out, gave themselves up and betrayed their leader, Captain Jack. He was the last man taken.

He, a few weeks later by the sentence of a military commission, suffered death together with a few of his principal men.

X

ALASKA INDIAN CHIEFS: FERNANDESTE, SITKA
JACK, AND ANAHOOTZ

ALASKA means great land, and, as you
can all see on the map, it is a great land
far west of Canada and north of the United
States. It was discovered in 1728 by Vitus
Bering, a Danish sailor in the Russian service,
and it belonged to Russia till 1867, when the
United States bought it for $7,200,000. This
country is so very far north that I am sure
if I asked you who lived there you would say
that the people must all be Eskimos, and you
are quite right, for Eskimos do live there, but
besides the Eskimos there are Indians who

live there, too. They are not as wild and war-like as the redmen further south, and are so willing to live as white men do that we have not needed to put them on reservations. Indeed, they would have given Uncle Sam no trouble at all but for the bad traders who would sell the Indians whisky, and no Indian is much good when he begins to like "fire water" better than anything else.

It was in 1875 that one of these Alaskan Indian chiefs, Fernandeste, was seized by some white men, made prisoner on board a steamer, and taken to Portland, Oregon. Some of the white men could talk Stickeen, the Indian language, and they frightened Fernandeste so much because he thought he would forever disgrace his people that he died before the ship reached land. Now the Indians loved this chief very much, and when the news came back his family was overcome with grief. All the Indians said they must

9

167

make the white men give them a great present for this bad treatment of Fernandeste or they would be cowards, and whatever happened his body must be brought back to Alaska.

Now at this time Uncle Sam had sent me, with a portion of the United States Army, to take care of the northwestern part of our country, so when I heard the story of Fernandeste I decided to go to Alaska and tell his friends how sorry I was and try to make them happy. It was vacation time, so my wife and children went along for a trip.

From Tacoma, on Puget Sound, we sailed to Victoria, the capital of British Columbia, and there went on board the steamer *California* for Alaska. What a glorious trip it was, sailing between rough-faced mountain sides, 3000 feet high, some snow-capped, some covered with feathery trees. Such a strange country, too, for the sun stayed up all night

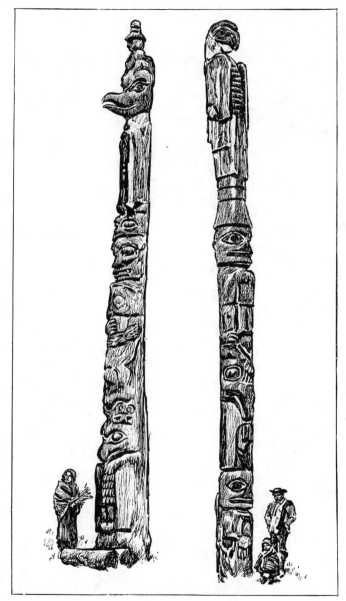

Alaska totem poles

and at ten o'clock I could read as well as at noon. My children did n't want to go to bed at all, and I remember what queer things we hung up at the windows to darken the rooms so the children could sleep.

At last one morning we anchored in a bay near an island and on that island was an army post called Fort Wrangel. There was a stockade around it made of the trunks of trees fifteen feet high, and there were heavy double gates made of logs fastened together. The commanding officer of the fort and Kalemste, sub-chief of the Wrangel Indians, came to meet us, and with them we went to the stockade. All the buildings of the fort were inside the stockade, and the officers and soldiers felt very safe when the gates were shut. Now some soldiers opened the gates for us to pass in. Kalemste and two other Indians were allowed to enter, but all the others turned back to their homes on the other end of the island.

These Wrangel Indians do not live in tepees and wigwams as the Indians further south, but in long houses made of immense planks split from large trees. A whole family—children, parents, grandparents, uncles, and aunts, and even some few friends live in one house. There is room enough in the middle on the ground to build fires and a small hole in the roof to let out some of the smoke. But the strangest things of all were the totem poles. In front of each house was a pole ten to thirty feet high. Animals were carved on the top and sides of the poles, sometimes a bird, a bear, or a fox. These totems are the signs of a tribe or family—just as we have the United States eagle, the English lion, the Scotch thistle, or French lily, but they certainly do look very funny standing in front of all the houses. One totem pole belonged to the chief, Fernandeste, and showed the tribe he belonged to among the Stickeen Indians, and the carvings gave a short history of his tribe. There were groves where the Indians danced together, and places where they worked when tanning and decorating the skins of animals, and where the children practised with bows and arrows, and it was all very different from any Indian villages I had seen before.

After we had our lunch at the fort, chairs were taken out in front of the stockade and the Indians gathered for a council. Kalemste stepped out in front of the Indians while his people crouched ready to listen. He told us the story of Fernandeste and how he had been invited on the steamer where some dreadful white men, who were prisoners being taken to Portland, Oregon, for selling liquor to the Indians at Wrangel, kept with the chief and frightened him so greatly that he died; and how his people wanted a potlash or present, so that the other Indians would not call them

173

cowards. I asked what would satisfy them and he replied, one hundred good blankets, only they must have their dead chief back again. Now a good warning had come to me before I started, and I was ready with permission from Uncle Sam. At a word the soldiers went into the stockade and then slowly returned bearing the body of Fernandeste back to those who loved him, and a hundred army blankets for the tribe. A sudden change came over the faces of the Indians, and taking the body from the soldiers they returned to their homes satisfied.

But Kalemste and a few of the leading men remained and asked if the chief of the white men would stay long enough to let him come early in the evening and give us a play. Indeed, we were all curious to see an Indian play, and as the captain of the ship could wait for us, I said yes.

In the evening we came together. The star-

The Indian village at Sitka

light was very bright and it was all still except for the washing of the sea on the shore.

The Indians came quietly, and without ado built a fire on the ground for a big torch to light us. The men were dressed fantastically, no two alike, and their arms and legs were painted. They gave first a dance of joy, which lasted over an hour. Then they showed in a rude way without speaking a word, simply by signs and motions, how Fernandeste went to the steamer, how he died, the crossing of the bar on the Columbia River, how his body was buried and taken again from the ground, and the return of it by the steamer to Wrangel; then our coming, our lunch and the council, but all so plainly shown that everybody knew what it meant and clapped their hands in applause for this fine acting.

Then Kalemste begged me to send them a teacher. He said the officers and soldiers had taught them a little, but they wanted a real

177

teacher. I promised, and the evening entertainment being over, we went on board our steamer and were soon sound asleep while the captain and crew watched and took us swiftly northward to Sitka.

When Alaska belonged to Russia they called Sitka New Arkangel, after a city in Russia, but we have called it by the Indian name Sitka. There were two bands of Indians here, one under Sitka Jack, the other under Anahootz. Anahootz came to see me in a soldier's coat and hat with a bright handkerchief about it. My boys were much amused at his appearance, but he was as dignified as a king, and presented to me a number of well-folded sheets of paper on each of which was the statement that Anahootz was a good Indian, a friend of the white men and the Indians, and told the truth. I went to see him in his home and he sat on a bench and gave me his only arm-chair. He told me he had thought much and spent many a night wide awake thinking what would be good for the Indians. Now he understood. He wanted peace between white men and Indians, under a good commander such as Major Campbell, the military governor. I told him his people seemed poor, but I thought if they would make baskets and belts and moccasins visitors would buy them. This pleased him, but he told me that most of all he wanted me to promise to send a teacher to them; that if I sent a good teacher his Indians would build a house, better than his own, for him. Of course I promised, and once more we boarded the *California* and started north to the mouth of Chilcat Creek.

The Chilcat Indians lived much like those at Sitka and Wrangel, but they had seen few white men. Here we found a stone four or five feet long and three feet thick, which the Indians said came from the moon. I suppose it was a meteorite, but the Indians said a great white man had asked them to protect and keep it till he came again, which they were glad to do.

Just as we were returning to the steamer we met Sitka Jack. He was the most famous chieftain in this region. Now he was in a long canoe filled with men, every man having a paddle in his hand, and eight or ten on each side. Sitka Jack with eagle feathers in his hat and a belt crammed full of pistols round his waist sat in the stern steering, a small United States flag in his hand. He was a very bright man, and after a little encouragement we had a good talk together. He told me that not many miles inland, if you went through Sitka Pass northward, there was a good level country where everything would grow and where there were very many people.

This was long ago, but since then many of our people have found their way to this great

A medicine-man of the Chilcat Indians

land of Alaska and have given riches to the United States in gold found in the Klondike and Yukon country. Men and women have taken the long journey to teach the Indian children, and under the shadow of the totem poles now are many men and women who were boys and girls when I first went to Alaska to tell those Indians that Uncle Sam was their friend.

XI

FAR in the Northwest of our country live the Chopunnish or Nez Percé Indians, a powerful tribe.

Chopunnish is an Indian word, but Nez Percé is French and means pierced noses. The name comes from the fact that these Indians used to pierce their noses and wear rings in them, just as some ladies we know pierce their ears and wear fine earrings.

The men of the tribe are large and tall and strong, and they are very proud and warlike. Every year they went far away, even one thousand miles, to hunt buffalo, while the

184

women planted little patches of Indian corn and the boys rode ponies or fished for salmon in the rivers. Now and then the Nez Percés fought, as all Indians do, and their enemies were especially the Blackfeet and Snakes, but they never killed a white man. Governor Stevens, one of the first white governors, gave these Indians a large tract of land bigger than New York State, where they lived and were very happy. After a while some missionaries came to live among them and started a big school where many Indian children studied and learned the white men's ways. Among these Indian children were two boys, the sons of a powerful chief called Old Joseph. Young Joseph and Ollicut went to the school for a short time, but while they were still very small their father became angry with another chief and moved off to Wallowa, a place far away on the Nez Percé reservation.

Then the white people began to see that this country was a good place to live in, and they asked Uncle Sam to give them some of it. Most of the Indians agreed to sell part of their big reservation and live on a part called the Lapwai lands, or reservation, but after this was arranged it was found that several bands of Nez Percés lived outside of this smaller reservation—the White Birds under their leader, White Bird; other Indians under a chief called Looking-Glass; several other bands, and some Indians led by Young Joseph, who had become their chief after Old Joseph died. These many bands of Nez Percés came together and made Young Joseph their chief. They said that the other Nez Percés had no right to sell their land, and that they did not wish to leave their homes.

In April, 1877, I took some soldiers and went to a fort near Walla Walla, Washington, many miles south of Fort Lapwai. Here I met

Chief Joseph in full costume

Ollicut, who came to represent his brother, who was sick. At his request I agreed to meet Joseph and his friends or Tillicums in twelve days at Lapwai, Idaho, and we all hoped that the meeting would result in a good peace. When I arrived at Fort Lapwai twelve days later an immense tent was ready for the council. Joseph, with about fifty Indians, had spent the night near by in handsome Indian lodges. His many ponies, watched by Indian lads, were feeding on the banks of Lapwai Creek. All was excitement, as with some officers I waited for the Indians to come that sunny morning to the "big talk." At last they came, riding slowly up the grassy valley, a long rank of men, all on ponies, followed by the women and children. Joseph and Ollicut rode side by side. The faces of all the Indians were painted bright red, the paint covering the partings of the hair, the braids of the warriors' hair tied with strips of white and scarlet. No weapons were in sight except tomahawk-pipes and sheath-knives in their belts. Everything was ornamented with beads. The women wore bright-colored shawls and skirts of cotton to the top of their moccasins.

They all came up and formed a line facing our square inclosure; then they began a song. The song was wild and shrill and fierce, yet so plaintive at times it was almost like weeping, and made us sorry for them, although we could not but be glad that there were not five hundred instead of fifty.

They turned off to the right and swept around outside our fence, keeping up the strange song all the way around the fort, where it broke up into irregular bubblings like mountain streams tumbling over stones.

Then the women and children rode away at a gallop and the braves, leaving their ponies, came in all in a single file with Joseph ahead.

They passed us each one formally shaking hands, and then we all sat down in the big tent. After a prayer I spoke to Joseph and told him that his brother Ollicut had said to me twelve days ago in Walla Walla that he wished to see me—now I was ready to listen to what he wished to say. Joseph then said that White Bird's Indians were coming; they were to be here soon and we must not be in a hurry, but wait for them. So we put off the "big talk" till the next day.

Again the Indians went through the same performance and again we were ready. White Bird had arrived and with a white eagle wing in his hand sat beside Joseph. Joseph introduced him to me, saying: "This is White Bird; it is the first time he has seen you." There was also an old chief, Too-hul-hul-sote, who hated white men. When they were seated again I told them that the President wanted them all to come up to Lapwai,

—to the part where nobody lived, and take up the vacant reservation, for the other lands had been given to the white men.

Joseph said: "Too-hul-hul-sote will speak."

The old man was very angry and said: "What person pretends to divide the land and put me on it?" I answered: "I am the man." Then among the Indians all about me signs of anger began to appear. Looking-Glass dropped his gentle style and made rough answers; White Bird, hiding his face behind that eagle wing, said he had not been brought up to be governed by white men, and Joseph began to finger his tomahawk and his eyes flashed. Too-hul-hul-sote said fiercely: "The Indians may do as they like, I am not going on that land."

Then I spoke to them. I told them I was going to look at the vacant land and they should come with me. The old man, Too-hul-hul-sote, should stay at the fort with the colonel till we came back. He arose and cried: "Do you want to frighten me about my body?" But I said: "I will leave you with the colonel," and at a word a soldier led the brave old fellow out of the tent and gave him to a guard.

Then Joseph quieted the Indians and agreed to go with me. We did not hasten our ride, but started after a few days. We then rode over forty miles together. Once Joseph said to me: "If we come and live here what will you give us—schools, teachers, houses, churches, and gardens?" I said, "Yes." "Well!" said Joseph, "those are just the things we do not want. The earth is our mother, and do you think we want to dig and break it? No, indeed! We want to hunt buffalo and fish for salmon, not plow and use the hoe."

"Yours is a strange answer," I said. After riding all over the country the Indians called it a good country, and they agreed to come and live there. The land was staked out, and Too-hul-hul-sote set free, and it was arranged that in thirty days all the outside Indians should be on the reservation, and we parted the best of friends.

Now, about this time Joseph's wife was taken sick, so he left his band and stayed away some distance with her in his lodge. While he was away some of the young warriors came to a farm-house and began to talk with two white men. For some reason they did not agree, and a young Indian tried to take a gun out of the farmer's hand. At once the farmer was frightened and called to the other white man for help. That white man ran up and began to shoot, killing the Indian. Now began all sorts of trouble. The Indians stole horses, burned houses, robbed travelers, and the whole country was wild with terror.

Joseph at first did not know what to do, but

A portrait of Chief Joseph on birch bark

General Howard and his good friend, Chief Joseph

at last he broke his agreement with me and all the outside Indians went on the war-path. For many months there were battles—battles —battles! Joseph was a splendid warrior, and with many of Uncle Sam's good soldiers he fought. I followed him for over fourteen hundred miles, over mountains and valleys, always trying to make him give up. At the last I sent two Nez Percé friends, "Captain John" and "Indian George" to Chief Joseph's strong place in the Little Rockies with a white flag to ask him to give up.

Joseph sent back word: "I have done all I can; I now trust my people and myself to your mercy."

So the surrender was arranged, and just before night on October 5, 1877, Joseph, followed by his people, many of whom were lame and wounded, came up to me and offered his rifle.

Beside me stood General N. A. Miles, who

197

had helped me and fought the last battle, and so I told Joseph that he, General Miles, would take the rifle for me.

Thus ended the great Nez Percé War, and Joseph went after a time to live with Moses, another chief of whom I will tell you some day.

Twenty-seven years later I met Chief Joseph, the greatest Indian warrior I ever fought with, at the Carlisle Indian School, and there he made a speech: "For a long time," he said, "I did want to kill General Howard, but now I am glad to meet him and we are friends!"

XII

MOSES, A GREAT WAR CHIEF WHO KNEW WHEN
NOT TO FIGHT

IN the Northwest of our great country there
are so many different tribes of Indians
that I cannot begin to tell you their names,
but they were often divided in this way: Those
who lived on reservations were called ''Reservation Indians'' and those who did not, ''Outside Indians.'' Now, Moses was chief of a
great many tribes of Outside Indians and he
was a very great chief. Of course, Moses was
not his Indian name, but Governor Stevens
gave it to him long ago and every one called
him so; indeed, he seemed to have forgotten
his Indian name and called himself Moses.

199

He was a very handsome man, tall and straight, and always well dressed. He usually wore a buckskin coat and trousers, and handsome beaded moccasins, and a broad, light felt hat with a thin veil encircling it. He always had a leather belt around his waist, in which he carried a long knife and pistol holster, the ivory pistol knob in plain sight.

Now, Moses had led his Indians in many battles, both against Indians and white men, and everybody knew that he was a brave warrior and could fight. Indeed, in 1858 one of the very fiercest battles we ever had with the Indians took place when Moses was the Indian war chief and General George Wright commanded the United States soldiers at the "Battle of Yakima River." But after Mr. Wilbur became the Indian Agent things changed, for the Indians loved him and called him Father Wilbur, and Moses decided not to fight the white men any more.

Many times Moses was asked to go on a reservation, but he always replied that he would live on a reservation, but not with Indians he did not know. Many tribes had asked him to be their chief, and he wanted "Washington" to give him the land in a bend of the Columbia River for a reservation. It was waste land, he said, where no white people wanted to live, but the Indians would be happy there, he knew. When Chief Joseph led the Nez Percés against us in the many battles I have told you about, he often sent to Moses to ask him to come and fight, too, but Moses always said, "No." Still this chief did not have an easy time, for many people said he was a bad Indian, and at last he wrote me a letter which I have kept many years and which I am sure you would like to see.

I Moses Chief want you to know what my tumtum is in regard to my tribes and the white people. Almost every day there come to me reports that the soldiers from Walla Walla are coming to take me away from this part of the country. My people are constantly excited and I want to know from you the truth so I can tell my people and have everything quiet once more among us. Since the last war we have had up here reports that I Moses am going to fight if the soldiers come; this makes my heart sick. I have said I will not fight and I say to you again I will not fight and when you hear the whites say Moses will fight, you tell them *no*. I have always lived here upon the Columbia River. I am getting old and I do not want to see my blood shed on my part of the country. Chief Joseph wanted me and my people to help him. His offers were numerous. I told him no—never. I watched my people faithfully during his war and kept them at home. I told them all when the war broke out that they should not steal; if any of them did I would report them to Father Wilbur. During all the past year I have not allowed any stranger Indians to come here fearing they would raise all excitement with my Indians. I am not a squaw—I know how to fight, but I tell you the truth. I do not want to fight and have always told my people so. It is about time to begin our spring work as we all raise lots of vegetables and wheat and corn and trade with Chinamen and get money.

I wish you would write me and tell me the truth so I can tell my people so they will be contented once more and go to work in their gardens. I do not want to go on the Yakima reservation as I told Colonel Watkins last summer. I wish to stay where I have always lived and where my parents died. I wish you would write to me and send by the bearer of this letter. And be sure I am a friend and tell you the truth.

Signed: Moses HIS X MARK Chief.

I replied that the Bannock Indians were giving me much trouble, but that when I got back I would arrange a meeting. In the meantime I would depend on him to keep peace.

Now, during this time it was hard for Moses, for two sets of Indians gave him trouble. The "Dreamers," led by Smoholly, tried to make Moses think that he should join many tribes and fight the white men, for, said they, all the Indians who have gone to the happy hunting-lands will rise from the dead before long and join us, so you must join, too. But Moses would not fight. Then some of those

Indians who were fighting crossed over the Columbia River and, finding a family by the name of Perkins living far from any settlement, killed every member of the family and burned their house and barn.

Some Indians told the white men that Moses was a friend of these dreadful warriors and was protecting them. The white people of Yakima City believed these idle tales and even accused Moses to me, but when I met him and we talked it over, he said that he would prove that what he said was true, for he would help find the three Cayuses Indians who had done this wrong and give them up to the Yakima Courts.

Always true to his word, he took with him thirty-five Indians and began to hunt. One evening Moses and his band camped for the night, and fearing no harm, were fast asleep, when a large body of white men surrounded them. These men seized Moses and bound him with cords, putting irons on his wrists, but still he would not fight and told all his Indians to point their rifles to the ground and offer no resistance. He said afterward that he gave up his pistol, knife, and gun and prepared to die, but instead he was taken to Yakima City and put in the jail or "Skookum House," as the Indians call it. Here Mr. Wilbur promised enough money to make them take off the irons, but still Moses was a prisoner. Then he said: "Let the one-armed soldier-chief (General Howard) know I am a prisoner: He is my friend and as soon as he knows it he will set me free." And this he constantly repeated. I was far away when the news reached me, but I came immediately and ordered that Moses be at once set at liberty, and I have never been sorry that I did so, for he was a true friend to the good white people, and by his simple word kept many hundred Indians at peace.

205

When he was free Moses asked again for a reservation, and at last it was given to him and to his people. There on the banks of the Columbia River he kept his people at peace and had them work farms and gardens.

The last time I saw him he visited me at Vancouver Barracks near Portland, Oregon, when, with many chiefs, he was on his way to Washington to visit the President of the United States. He was a brave war chief and not afraid to fight, though he had learned to know that peace is best.

XIII

LIKE the great Montezuma of old Mexico, Chief Winnemucca, who was born and lived the most of his life beside Pyramid Lake, Nevada, had a thinking mind and a large, warm heart. He was chief of an Indian nation called the "Piutes," and before any white men came over the Rocky Mountains to disturb them, there were several thousand Indians, to whom he was like a father. He saw to it that they had plenty of good food to eat, nice furs and skins to wear, and handsome tepees (or wigwams) for their families to live in. He had a good wife and many children of his own; he was always very kind to them, and took much pains to teach all he

207

himself knew to his eldest son, who was to be Chief Winnemucca after him.

Seventy years ago the Piutes were a peace-loving and contented people. They knew how to gather in the swift antelopes from the plains, how to catch the deer and ensnare the wild turkeys, and help themselves to all the game of the mountains round about their broad valley and clear lake in which they caught splendid speckled trout and other choice fish. The Piutes never appeared to be as shrewd and smart as the Snake Indians, and they were not warlike; yet with their bows and arrows they did drive off the thieves that came from their Indian neighbors, some-times, to hunt in the mountains or fish in the lake.

Chief Winnemucca taught the Piutes very different lessons from other Indian chiefs; for example, to love peace and make constant effort to keep it; always to be kind one to another; always to tell the truth, and never to take for one's self what belonged to another; to treat old people with tender regard; to care for and help the helpless; to be affectionate in families and show real respect to women, particularly to mothers; yet he and his Piutes had no books, no writing, no chairs, no furniture, almost none of those common articles that make our houses so comfortable. Chief Winnemucca, from time to time, had wonderful dreams. One night he dreamed that some people who were different from the red men, would by and by come from the east; that they would be finer people than any he had ever seen, and that their faces would be of a white color, bright and beautiful. He stretched out his hands toward them and said: "My white brothers!"

Some time before the great explorers, Lewis and Clark, crossed the plains and saw Chief Winnemucca's valley, a company of hunters from Canada came. They were usually named *Voyageurs,* and were trying to collect precious furs. They hunted and trapped the beavers and foxes or bought skins from the Indians. Then these voyageurs would carry the furs to the nearest trading places and sell them at a good price to white traders.

One day a party of these voyageurs came to a high plateau and, sitting on their hardy ponies, looked for the first time on Pyramid Lake. They were taking in the beauty of the scene when suddenly a few Indians, riding furiously toward them, halted suddenly, and one Indian rode forward, making signs of good-will as he approached. But the hunters were frightened and caught up their guns, though they did not fire. At this the Indian hurried away, joined the others, and they all dashed into the woods and rode as fast as they could straight to Chief Winnemucca's wigwam. As soon as the venturesome Piute, much excited, had told all he knew about the appearance of strangers up there on the eastern plateau, asserting that they were well mounted on large ponies, that they were curiously dressed, and that they surely had white faces, Winnemucca cried out with joy: "They are my white brothers!" and after a few moments added: "I knew you would come; you are the white brothers of my dream."

Chief Winnemucca hastened with twenty of his Indians to meet the traders. All the Indians were mounted on little ponies adorned with cedar sprigs and some bright flowers fastened to their manes and tails. The Indians were afraid and kept close together, but the chief was happy and rode boldly ahead to meet his white brothers. Now the voyageurs were full of fear and, firing their guns in the air, motioned for the Piutes to stop. These unfriendly signs startled Winnemucca. His heart bled as he saw his men hanging back in terror; but he could not forget his beautiful dream, so for a while he tried to draw nearer the strangers. They shouted angrily at him; but he got down from his saddle fifty or sixty yards away, put his strong bow and quiver of arrows on the ground, and spread out his arms as a sign of peace; but the white men, believing him and his followers to be treacherous because they were wild Indians, would not let them come any closer. Now Chief Winnemucca had heard about some powder guns which warlike Indians had and he instinctively recognized these white men's rifles as weapons of war. Greatly disappointed, he and his party rode back to their pretty village, and next morning the voyageurs passed on westward. The Piutes never saw them again.

It was not very long after this visit when

"He spread out his arms as a sign of peace"

another party of about fifty white men descended from the same plateau and encamped two miles below Pyramid Lake on the bank of a swift running river.

Again the good chief went down as he had done before and tried his best by peace signs to welcome the strangers, but they would not let an Indian approach them. They even fired from loaded rifles to frighten the Piutes away. This time the Indians saw where the bullets struck the trees and bushes. But Winnemucca, after the white men had gone, reflected upon the cause of the white brothers' fear of them. So he said: "I will not give them up, I will show them a brother's heart."

He took a few of his principal men and had them bring with them their women and children. They followed the white men several days and encamped every night in plain sight. At last the white leader, prompted by his guide who knew something of Indian ways,

215

decided that the Piutes meant them no harm. Little by little they talked by signs. The Indians showed them how to avoid bad trails and made some short cuts in their journey and always led them to the finest camping places where they could have plenty of wood and good water. Every night they brought them a deer or an antelope. The leader of the white people was a generous and good man, so he and Chief Winnemucca soon became friends. After this success, which delighted his heart, the chief and his followers returned to their home on Pyramid Lake.

The next company of white people going toward California were more numerous. With them was the American pathfinder, Capt. John C. Frémont, and he and Winnemucca communicated right away. They first met where the Union Pacific Railway now crosses the Truckee River—called by the Piute Indians Truckee because it means "all right.'' Frémont took a particular liking to the warm-hearted chief, and he asked him to lead a party of Piute scouts. The scouts consisted of the chief and eleven picked Indian men, and from that time Winnemucca was called Captain Truckee or All-Right. With Frémont, these Indians went all the way to California, and helped him while there in his contests with the Mexicans. They learned after a fashion to speak English, and Winnemucca could always make an American understand him. He was proud of his English, but prouder of a piece of tough paper on which Frémont had written a recommendation of Captain Truckee. This the chief always called "My Rag Friend."

Chief Winnemucca liked California so much that he decided after much thinking and talking with his people to go back to that beautiful and fruitful land. His son, who was to be the chief, Winnemucca Second, was put in charge of the Piutes left behind, while Captain Truckee took thirty families with him for the long journey. Of his own family he took his wife, his daughter-in-law, and four of her children—they were named by their grandfather a little later: Natchez, Lee, Mary, and Sarah, two boys and two girls. Sarah, who was then six years old, was the youngest, and her grandfather's favorite, and he always spoke of her as "my sweetheart." She was dreadfully afraid of white men, and would hide her face, so as not to see them, and weep a long time if one spoke to her. The cause of this terror was that she once heard her father say the Piutes were to have great sorrows and troubles from bad whites.

A sister of charity succeeded in winning her heart. The result of this good lady's friendship was that Mary and Sarah learned to speak English, and for a short term were taken into the Catholic boarding-school, but the feeling against all Indians among the whites was such that they declared they would take away all their children if Indians were allowed to come there. In California Mr. Scott employed Captain Truckee and his Indians to care for numerous herds of cattle and horses, and the Indians on their ponies were most faithful and successful herdsmen.

The chief, after about a year in California, heard that the sub-chief (his son, Winnemucca Second) and all the Piutes with him, had had great trouble. At first two white settlers on their way west had been waylaid in the mountains, and robbed and killed with arrows. The arrows were left there and had on them the Washoes' marks, but the white people insisted that Piutes and the Washoes were all the same. Again two wicked white men carried off two little Piute girls and hid them. After a long search the two Indian fathers found them in a cellar, bound with cords. The

219

Indians became enraged at this and killed the white men.

Besides, a large party of white people came to Pyramid Lake as others had done before them. It was quite late in the fall of the year and Winnemucca Second with most of his Indians was away hunting in the mountains. The Indians had left their winter supply of seeds, nuts, wild onions, and camas, and a large quantity of dried deer-meat and salted fish, carefully stored away near the Truckee River. The strangers helped themselves to what they could use, and burned up all the remaining food.

Winnemucca Second became alarmed at this, and when a volunteer company came to punish the Piute Indians for the loss of the white settlers, he and his followers began to lose all confidence in the "white brothers" that his good father had always trusted and defended. So the sub-chief kept all of the Piutes he could get to stay with him in different camps in the mountains.

Hearing all this the old chief left his two grandsons to work for Mr. Scott in California and, taking with him his daughter-in-law and the two girls, Mary and Sarah, in a large wagon, guarded by several of his Indians, he drove five hundred miles back to Pyramid Lake. He sent a messenger to find his son and begged him to come back to the beautiful valley and have his people come with him. Here they met the chief, and the wise and good-hearted old man spoke for his white brothers, and once more taught his people useful lessons.

Beside the beautiful lake he lived for many years, and when at last he was about to pass over to the Happy Land he called his son to him and told him never to forget his duty to his own people and to love and always be kind to his white brothers.

221

XIV

TOC-ME-TO-NE, AN INDIAN PRINCESS

WE called her Sarah Winnemucca, but her real name was Toc-me-to-ne, which means shell-flower. Have you ever seen these flowers growing in an old garden among their many cousins of the Mint family? Well, Toc-me-to-ne loved them of all flowers best, for was she not herself a shell-flower?

Her people were Piute Indians, and they lived in every part of what is now the great State of Nevada.

Toc-me-to-ne had a flower name, so she was allowed to take part in the children's flower festival, when all the little girls dance and sing, holding hands and making believe that they are the very flowers for which they are

222

named. They wear their own flowers, too, and after they have sung together for a while one will dance off on the grass by herself while all the boys and girls look on and she sings:

> I am a daisy gold and white,
> Somebody catch me—me!

The grown-up people watch, too, as their children play, and Toc-me-to-ne was never happier than when, light as a bird, she danced and sang her shell-flower song:

> See me! see me, a beautiful flower.
> Give me a hand and dance.

Then after the plays and dancing the children had all sorts of good things to eat, and the flower festival was over for a year.

Only three times did Toc-me-to-ne take part in the flower festival, for when she was quite a little girl her grandfather, Chief Winnemucca, took his family and went to live in California, and when they came back she was almost grown up.

Her grandfather was very fond of her, and called her sweetheart, so she was sad and lonesome indeed when he left her and went to the Happy Spirit Land; but she did not forget his last words to her before he went. "Sweetheart," he said, "do not forget my white brothers; be kind to them and they will be kind to you and teach you many things."

In California the old chief gave to his grandchildren new names—Natchez, Lee, Mary, and Sarah, and Sarah learned to speak fairly good English. Later, when she came to Pyramid Lake, she played with Mr. Ormsby's children and learned to speak better English. Besides this Mrs. Ormsby taught her to cook and sew and to do housework.

When Sarah was fifteen years old she made the long five-hundred-mile journey to California once more with her brothers and sister and her grandmother. Her brothers took care of cattle for good Mr. Scott, who had known and loved Chief Winnemucca, and he gave them good wages, several fine horses, and two ponies for Sarah and Mary to ride. The sisters had always ridden bareback like Indian men, but when Christmas came Sarah was surprised to find a beautiful Mexican side-saddle from her brother Lee, and she learned to ride like the white ladies, and was very proud and happy.

Now the Piutes always would wander about. They lived by hunting and fishing, not by farming, and so they moved from place to place wherever there was game. When they were in the mountains rough white settlers came to Pyramid Lake and caught almost all of the fish with nets, so that there were no fish when the Indians returned. This made the Indians angry, and so trouble began. All this time Sarah was in California, her father, Chief Winnemucca Second, and her mother were in Nevada, and she often heard good

225

news from them; but one spring when she was seventeen years old two Indians came bringing the news from her father that he was in the mountains and wanted all his children to come to him, but especially Sarah.

Starting on their ponies they began the journey, riding beside the wagon where the grandmother rode. It took twenty-five days to reach Carson City, but here their father and mother met them, and next day all went to see Governor Nye, where Sarah told in English what her father, the chief, wanted to say.

Governor Nye was very jolly and good, and when he knew how things really were he told the white settlers not to interfere with the Indians, and sent soldiers from the fort to drive the rough men away. So Governor Nye and Chief Winnemucca became good friends as they never could have been but for little Toc-me-to-ne and her bright interpretations.

The Princess Sarah

For the next year Sarah talked both Piute and English, and settled many little troubles. She was called friend both by the Indians and soldiers, and her father and she thought often of old Chief Winnemucca's words and kept peace with their white brothers.

But just as storm-clouds gather, so whispers came that there would be war between the soldiers and the Piutes. One day some old men were fishing in a lake when cavalry soldiers rode up and fired at them. The Indians ran to their tepees near by, but the soldiers followed and hurt some of them. The captain of the soldiers thought they belonged to a band of bad Indians, and as he spoke only English none could explain. As soon as they understood the dreadful mistake, of course, every one was very sorry and did what he could to make it right. One of Sarah's little sisters was badly hurt, but Chief Winnemucca and Sarah only spoke sadly of the

12   229

"Lake Harney trouble," and were still friendly to the white people.

About this time Sarah came down to Muddy Lake to help her brother Natchez, who was sub-chief there. Nearby, Mr. Nugent, the Indian agent, had a big store, where he sold all sorts of things. Now Uncle Sam did not allow agents to sell shot and gunpowder to the Indians, but one day Mr. Nugent did sell some to a Piute Indian. The Indian rode away across the river very happy, but soon one of Mr. Nugent's men met him. He saw the shot and powder and in English told the Indian to give them up. Of course the Indian could not understand and tried to ride on, then the white man fired and shot him. The dreadful news spread among all the Indians and they were very angry, and said Mr. Nugent must die, because they believed he had let the Piute have the powder and then sent his man to shoot him on his way.

Angry Indians rushed to Natchez and frightened women and children gathered around Sarah, but they both mounted their swift ponies and hurried away to save the agent's life if possible. The river at the ford was high. Sarah's pony stumbled in the swift current and threw her off, but her brother helped her to remount, and in her wet clothes, she galloped on to Mr. Nugent's house. When Sarah saw him she cried to him to get quickly away or the Indians would kill him, but he replied that he was not afraid and called to his men to get their guns, saying he would show the rascals how to fight. Natchez and Sarah begged him to go away till they could quiet the angry Indians, but he would not and told them to leave him. There was nothing else to do, but at the ford they met the angry Indians and stopped them. Natchez called a council in his tepee, and here he and Sarah succeeded in quieting the excitement for a time. Soon afterward word came that two white men herding horses near a place called Deep Wells had been shot by the brothers of the Piute Indian who bought the powder. Then Mr. Nugent went to Fort Mc-Dermit to get soldiers to punish the Indians.

Now when the agent asked for soldiers the captain, who was a wise man, decided to know the truth first, so he sent two friendly Indians with a letter to Sarah. This is the letter:

MISS SARAH WINNEMUCCA: Your agent tells us very bad things about your people killing two of our men. I want you and your brother Natchez to meet me at our place to-night. I want to talk to you and your brother.

(signed) CAPTAIN JEROME,
Company M, 8th U. S. Cavalry.

The Indians were terrified when Sarah told them what was in the letter and said: "Write, write; you may be able to save us from a dreadful war." Sarah had nothing to write with, but she said: "I will try," and with a sharp-pointed stick and some fish blood scratched off this letter:

HON. SIR: My brother is not here. I am looking for him every minute. We will go as soon as he comes in. If he comes to-night we will come some-time during the night.

Yours,

S. W.

The messengers were hardly gone when Natchez and his men returned. They took fresh horses and he and Sarah started for the fort. She says: "We went like the wind, never stopping till we got there." When they arrived, the wicked agent was with Captain Jerome, but Sarah told the whole story, and the Captain treated them well and promised to do what was right. Then the brother and sister, tired as they were, rode back to their tepee on Muddy Lake. The next day a good officer and some soldiers came and camped near them. The soldiers gave the Indians food and guarded them while Sarah and Natchez held meetings with their people and showed them how kind the soldiers had been. After this, because of the bad ways of Nugent, the commander at Fort McDermit had Natchez and many Indians come to the army post and pitch their tepees. Sarah lived with her brother and his wife, and was the interpreter and peacemaker; and she persuaded the chief, her father, to get together as many as possible of the wandering Piutes and bring them to the fort.

Sarah was sweet and handsome and very quick and able. When she grew older she married one of the young army officers, but later he went East and she returned to her own people and lived on the Malheur Indian Reservation. Here she was always called "the Princess" because of her influence over her people.

It was in 1878 that the Bannock Indians started on the warpath in Idaho and, joining the Malheur Piutes, fought the white people wherever they went. This was called the Piute and Bannock War. The Princess, Sarah Winnemucca, was riding near Fort Lyons, Idaho, when she heard of the trouble. She was on her way to a railway station at Elko, Nevada, hoping to go to Washington to try and have some wrongs put right on the Malheur agency. When she heard the news she at once turned back and went to the sheep ranch near Boise City, and when I heard she was there I telegraphed to Captain Bernhard who was nearby with some soldiers, to ask the "Princess" to go as a messenger of peace to the angry Indians. She said she would go, and, taking with her some true Indian friends, she rode, in a day and a half, over one hundred miles. She was approaching the Indian camp in the dark and wondering how to get in unnoticed when she heard a sound. She called and an answering sign showed her it was an In-

235

dian. To her surprise and delight it proved to be her own brother, Lee Winnemucca. They had a long talk, and Sarah changed her usual neat dress for an old skirt and Indian blanket, painting her face and pulling a shawl over her head like the squaws. Then she went straight into the Indian camp and to her father's lodge among the fighting warriors who never thought for a moment of what she was there for. When she saw her father she had a long talk with him in the Piute language, and begged him not to have war with his white brothers. Of course the Bannock Indians could not understand what she said, so they suspected nothing. As soon as it was dark Sarah went out quietly into the woods and waited. One by one Chief Winnemucca and his family with many of his followers stole out of the camp and joined her. Then she guided them to the sheep ranch, and there I met them three days after I had sent my telegram. With her sister-in-law Mattie for a companion, this Indian Princess, Sarah Winnemucca, became my guide, messenger, and interpreter till the close of that fearful Piute and Bannock War.

She did our government great service, and if I could tell you but a tenth part of all she willingly did to help the white settlers and her own people to live peaceably together I am sure you would think, as I do, that the name of Toc-me-to-ne should have a place beside the name of Pocahontas in the history of our country.

XV

MATTIE, THE DAUGHTER OF CHIEF SHENKAH

CHIEF SHENKAH was a Piute Indian like the first Chief Winnemucca, whom the white men, who early traveled over the Rocky Mountains, met on the broad prairie land of Nevada. He was one of Winnemucca's young followers. Of noble appearance and always brave and trustworthy, Shenkah became the chief of a small tribe of the Piutes, after Winnemucca's death. When the Piutes were at peace with other Indians and with the white people, Shenkah was very friendly indeed, especially to the soldiers, and our officers were much pleased when they could, on marches in search of lakes and rivers round their camps and posts, get

238

Shenkah for a guide. He hunted deer and other game for them and they gave him a rifle and trusted him to make long journeys into the mountains. He always returned, and never without different kinds of wild game.

After his old chief went far away to California with General Fremont, trouble arose on account of a sad mistake which resulted in a dreadful war between some of the soldiers and the Indians. Chief Shenkah, leading his warriors, was in that war from the beginning to the end, until, at last, a good peace came.

His daughter, Mattie, when about twenty years of age, told me about her father. Mattie could read and write English slowly, and spoke it well enough for me to understand her. She talked with a pretty musical tone, each sentence sounding sometimes like a song, and sometimes her sentences were like

239

poetry. This is what she said: "My first mem'ry is 'way back. It is like a shadow, a dream. I just see him, my father! I have this picture of him, very sad, very sad, in my heart. I did not know much then, not much as I do now. He was so strange,—so different from all the rest. I know now that he was strange because he was just leaving us—for always. Oh, I was such a little girl! My father had been hurt in battle; he was very pale, and his eyes very bright, and looking far away. I am sure he knew when he spoke to me that he could not live to see another sun. He was lying down on the ground, and he took me and pressed me tenderly in his arms against his breast. Chief Egan, my uncle, was kneeling by my father's side and bending over us with tears in his eyes. At last my dear father spoke and said: 'Egan, my brother, the Great Spirit calls me away— I must go. I cannot take my little child with

240

me—the Great Spirit does not call her to go now. I wish I could take her with me to meet her mother; but I cannot. My brother, I leave her to you, be her father.' Such words I am sure, for they pressed on my mem'ry, are the ones my poor dear father used. They were wonderful and so have remained with me through all my years. My uncle, Chief Egan, gave my father an answer, but I do not quite remember what he said, but he laid his hand very gently on my head while my father added a few words which, like his others, have always been in my mind: 'My daughter, my little dove, you cannot know what this parting means; to me it is a bitter one, but you and I will meet again; your good Uncle Egan will be a father to you and you must be a good daughter to him.' After a few minutes of silence he gave his last words: 'Now I go in peace.' "

This is all that Mattie could remember.

241

She went away to live with her uncle, who became a chieftain among the Piutes, and who led many of them in the pursuits of peace and of war. He was kind and loving to his adopted daughter, and she returned his love with childlike devotion and always treated him as a father.

It was perhaps two years after the death of her father when she was carried to a camp called Howluk near the borders of Nevada. There had been just then some battles between the white people and the Indians, and the Indians had been again defeated. This war would not have come on if the white men and the Indians had spoken the same language and could have understood each other, and when Mattie told me of it, she said: "When will my red brothers learn that it is more than foolish to rise up and go on the war-path against our white brothers? Even now we are reading and hearing of

242

war. We poor women and the innocent little children and the old and helpless are the ones who suffer most. But now I know that the white men make war with their white brothers also. Why is this? Why do they make war with each other and make us suffer? Oh, we suffer so much; not only our bodies by hunger, sickness, cold, or heat, but our hearts bleed from the moment our dear ones go away under the sound of the song or the band and the drum. Then comes the terrible time of waiting—my breath seems to stop when I remember it. Then there is the news of wounds and death to reach us at home; very few can follow the cry of their hearts to run to the beloved one, because there are little ones to keep them at home."

She went on to say: "I learned about wars at school in Oregon, and, as you know, I was again and again in war myself, and it is horrid! I am no coward-girl, and I am

243

not afraid even when the guns fire; but I do not want war. Men who are so wise as to make so many wonderful things should find a way to settle their troubles without causing so much wretchedness and sorrow and tears. I am only a poor Indian girl, and though I 've been to school many days, yet I know but very little. I am sure that many of my white sisters, who know more than I do, think about battles and wars just as I do.''

In a letter to Mrs. Parish, a lady who was very much beloved by the Piute Indians, she writes: ''My uncle called all his Indians around him and spoke to them in this way: 'The white men are taking away from us all our land here in Nevada. They are driving off all our ponies. The war-chief of the Pi-utes was angry, and he had already taken the war-path. He, Chief Shenkah, was my brother, as you know. He did not succeed. The red man and white man did fight many suns, many soldiers and many braves fell in battle, and the young men are buried all along the creeks and rivers. My brother, Chief Shenkah has passed on to the better land. We see very plainly that the red men cannot fight the white men. We have not such good rifles and good horses as they have. Our bows and arrows are nothing. And now the white men say *Peace*. They say, take a home in Malheur, Oregon. There is good land, good water, and plenty of food over there. The red man and the white man must eat bread together. I now say this is good,— let us go. Egan is done.'

"Young as I was, I do not forget the long ride we took to Malheur. My people were very poor. Many of them were ill on the way from the want of clothing and good food; but as my uncle, Chief Egan, had decided that it was best to go, the braves of the tribe kept up from day to day the weary journey. A large number had to go on foot, as at that time the ponies, which remained to us after the war, were very few, and those we had were mostly thin of flesh, and many lame. My good Uncle Egan never forgot me. He gave me all I needed, and I had a nice little mouse-colored pony to carry me. The pony was one of the best among them all, and so he had to bear some goods as well as me. The bundles were put on his back and tied fast before I was put up on top of them. As I have now seen an elephant, I think that my little horse looked very much like a small elephant. His legs seemed very short. I was a little afraid, but Uncle Egan kindly strapped me to the load, and with pleasant words handed me a small whip and remarked that I was high up, higher than all the other riders, so I was quite safe and proud. At times, as ponies will, mine would stop beside the trail and put down his head

An Indian Horse-Race

to eat, then I would use my whip, though he
appeared to know that my whippings did not
mean a great deal. Our ponies seemed to
know about everything much more than
those of the white people. Some would not
let a white man mount them. They showed
their disgust in a very plain way—hard to
catch, and, being caught, hard to bridle, twist-
ing their heads one way and another. Oh,
how I used to enjoy the fun watching a pale-
face in his vain attempts to subdue one of
our horses who was perfectly gentle with any
of us Indians. Think of the saddling! By
a wicked little shake of his body the blanket
would slip off, first on one side and then on
the other, and the saddle go forward or back-
ward. The best part of the fun was to look
at the white man's attempt to mount an Indian pony; with the saddle on he would think
all was right, and get one foot nearly into
the stirrup, when the nag would move just

a little bit, then another little bit, just enough to make his rider hop after him on one foot. To us children all this appeared so amusing that we greeted the effort with shouts of laughter. Such things happened to me when I was quite little. At school I learned that it was very unkind and rude so to laugh—to laugh at any one; but I think the children could not well help it, because here was a little animal which any Indian child five years old could catch by the mane, lead to a log, jump on and ride wherever he pleased. Of course our little nags had their likes and dislikes, just like ourselves. I think we were a little proud to find that these white men, who brought such wonderful things to us, were not equal to us in training and riding ponies.

"On that long march to Malheur we had an old donkey. His name was Wee-choo. I was such a naughty Indian child that I enjoyed Wee-choo's mischievous performances, as I afterward enjoyed what I saw in a regular circus. I used to give hearty cheers for our old donkey. No white man or white woman ever could succeed in riding him, though many frontiermen and boys tried to do so. At one time they came great distances and had the ambition to ride what they called 'Egan's donkey.' At every race or Indian feast this donkey was a source of great merriment. He would put himself in every ridiculous posture and always managed to send a white man flying from his back.

"At one time there came a tall, long-limbed Irishman. His legs, if he ever could have sat on Wee-choo's back, were so long that his feet would have touched the ground. He looked like a grasshopper when trying to get on. The nearest he ever came to it caused him to jump entirely over the donkey and sit flat on the ground amid the laughing and shouting of the Indians. No one was

251

ever badly hurt and Wee-choo was a great favorite with us. You may understand that some soft old river-bed or other very sandy place was chosen for the Wee-choo circus. With the Indians the old animal became so tame that no mother in our tribe would hesitate for a moment to put her child on his back, where he would sit up straight, if strong enough, and hold to his mane. I remember the kindness of the children to this old donkey. They gave him milk to drink after his teeth became too decayed to eat grass or hay. We would grind his barley, corn or wheat, and soak it for him, and he appeared to understand and appreciate our care.''

At last, after the long and tedious journey, Chief Egan and his Indians reached Malheur. They were put on a large piece of land called a reservation—something very few of the tribe knew anything about. It appeared to the people something they did not like, some sort of prison.

Mattie said: "Had my uncle, Chief Egan, seen any other way to provide for his people, he never would have gone there, and would never have used his influence to bring them all to that place. But what were they to do? All our land in Nevada that was of any account had been taken away and settled upon by the white people. Every place which we had held and where there was good soil and good water was taken and fenced in as a white man's claim; and so we came to Malheur, Oregon. I have been told that the word 'Malheur' means misfortune, and as soon as the people heard this meaning, it added to their homesickness and sadness."

But Mattie was fortunate. She met Mrs. Parish. No white person had ever spoken so kindly to her, nor looked so pleasantly in her face. Mattie's heart went out to this good woman. She did not then quite understand her language, but she did understand her gentle voice and kind manner. Again Mattie found a loving welcome from the interpreter, Sarah Winnemucca, who soon became a sister to her and a teacher. Mr. Parish was, at that time, in charge of all the Indians, and he was of such noble spirit and kind ways, that he very soon made them feel that Malheur was not so bad for them as they first had feared.

Mattie (her teacher, Mrs. Parish, says) looked very quaint and nice in her manta dress; and how good and attentive she was in the school! She also remembered the pretty flowers that Mattie brought her, and how radiant she was when told that her good friend loved flowers, and put them into a vase on her desk. Mattie loved her teacher more every day, and this loving little girl was dearest of all to her teacher.

Mattie loved to talk of those days when

the Indians had Mr. Parish for their good agent. One day, as the children came into the school-room their attention was attracted by a great number of beautiful colored pictures hung on the walls of the room—pictures of horses, dogs, cats, birds, trees, and many things which they had never seen before. Mattie says that the little Indians were as happy as they could be when they looked upon those pictures for the first time. The pictures were so attractive that their school-room soon filled with children, children large and small, and the largest did not know more than the smallest.

One day Chief Egan came in and said to the scholars: "You must be very good children and obey the teacher; give good attention to what she says and remember it as well as you can. The great father in Washington sent her to teach the little ones, and this was good for us."

No Indian chief seemed to be more respected and loved by his people than Chief Egan. Mattie remembered the day when she tried hard and at last succeeded in lisping the teacher's name. The next day she learned to say "Good morning," and all the children were soon able to say, "Good morning, Mother Parish."

Mr. Parish one day brought in and hung near the teacher's desk a clear-faced clock. It was the first one that these children had ever looked upon, and it took them two or three days to get used to it, first, to call it by name in English and then, little by little, to learn, as they all did, how to tell the time of day.

At this school Mattie had a little boy friend named Tayhue. "Poor little fellow," she said, "he was so good and stupid, trying so hard, as hard as ever he could, but somehow letters and words would not sound right out of his mouth. No one could picture Tayhue's sounds. Well, he never spoke quite plainly in his own language." Mattie said that one should see him now, that he has grown up into a very nice young man and has married. He married little La-loo, and he declared that he loved her from the time she tried to teach him what to say in school.

When Mattie could speak English she said to Mrs. Parish: "You know I have no mother, so I had more love to give you than the other children. Did you ever dream how very dear you were to me? As soon as you thought that we children could understand you told us about the Saviour. I would think of all you said to us when I went home, and from your words there came most sweet and lovely thoughts to me,—indeed, you woke up my soul."

Mattie describes the time when the large maps came and were shown near the teacher's desk. She recalled particularly the great map of the United States. There were many different colors to represent the States, and at first the children thought that the land must be red, green, yellow, or blue, just as it looked to them on the map. They had hard work to understand the picture of the ocean. Mattie had seen several lakes, but not till by and by, when she came to San Francisco, did she see the grand sight.

When Mattie grew up she became the wife of Lee Winnemucca, and when I saw her,— as I often did during the last year of her short life,—she was always with Lee's sister Sarah, doing what she could to help and comfort her people, for they had suffered many trials and hardships during the Piute and Bannock War. She had not forgotten her early lessons at Malheur, and by her sweet manners and loving spirit made every one about her very happy.

XVI

THE Indians pronounced the name of Egan, Ehegante; but the soldiers and the white men living near the Indians' reservation, situated in eastern Oregon, called him Egan.

Egan was born a Umatilla. His father and mother were both from the Cayuse tribe who lived in the valley of the beautiful Umatilla River. That river flows from the springs and creeks of the lofty Blue Hills of Oregon, and with a length of about forty miles coursing westward, enters the Columbia River, not far south of the old Fort Walla Walla, where is now the little village of Wallula.

When very small, Egan's father and mother, with several other Cayuses, were away from home out on a meadow gathering wild onions and other kinds of nature's food. They had in their camp of tepees men, women, and children. Suddenly a wild war party of Indians from the Snake country came upon them and a fierce battle occurred. All the Cayuses in the camp were killed except the children. These children were carried off and scattered among the Snakes and the Piutes. Little Egan was left with and brought up by a good Piute family.

When he was old enough, he became famous among the young Indian hunters. He was above the medium height, very handsome, strong, and athletic; could lead any party in fishing the streams, climbing the mountains or chasing the deer. He could not have been more than twenty when he married the sister of Shenkah, a Piute chief. This chief called

An Indian Encampment

him brother. Side by side with Shenkah he had fought against hostile tribes of Indians and against the white settlers and soldiers under our General Crook, till he himself became a well-known war-chief.

While Winnemucca the second was the acknowledged chief of all the tribes of the Piute nation, Egan held the headship of a tribe in 1872, which, about that time, left Nevada and journeyed several hundred miles to Malheur, eastern Oregon. Before this, Egan's tribe was not a very settled people, under no real control; composed in great part of wild, roving, half-starved bands, off in the mountain districts, far from white farmers, and depending for their living on hunting, fishing, and, too often, on stealing the sheep and cattle of the settlers.

In the winter of 1872 and 1873, when the snows were deep, there were then at Malheur about a thousand Indians, Piutes mainly; but some were Bannocks and some of the Snake-River tribe.

In 1874 they had an excellent agent, Major Sam Parish. He and Chief Egan soon became the best of friends. In the spring, Parish set apart twenty acres of good ground, and tried to teach the Indians, hardly wiser than untaught children, how to cultivate the land and raise crops. Through Egan the Indians came to love Major Parish, while in a school for the little ones Mrs. Parish more than seconded her husband's efforts. At the start they were awkward and slow to learn practical farming, but soon they made progress, for they had promised Egan that they would do their best. Over and over again the agent showed them just the right way to plow and harrow, furrow and plant, till perseverance won the day. Before very long they saw the result of their labor in fields full of corn, potatoes, squashes, onions, and turnips, and all this product was to be their own. But the best part of the trial was: "The Piute would work!"

In 1876, more than one hundred acres were covered with fine crops, and the Indians had done the good work themselves, and were reaping the reward. The Indians at this time, as a rule, were contented and happy, with the exception of a few unruly ones led by a "dreamer" named Oytes. He called himself a "medicine-man," and his influence was much like that of all the other medicine-men among the Indians. They always had some queer ways of thinking and acting. Quick-witted, ugly in appearance, and strange in their conduct, they would frighten men and women by their claims of supernatural powers.

Oytes said: "I can defeat all our enemies! No bullet can hurt me. I have the power to kill any of you! It is wrong to dig up the face of the earth,—the earth is our mother; we must live upon what grows of itself,'' etc., etc.

After a few days Major Parish was told by the good-hearted Egan about Oytes—how wicked he was; how discontented he made many of the Indians; and how idle and worthless many became from his example and his teaching; furthermore, he planned to assassinate the agent and Egan. At last Parish sent for Oytes and said to him in the presence of his friends: ''I have three hundred dollars in a bank. If you will stand up before me and let me fire a bullet from this gun straight at your breast, and if it passes through your body and does not hurt you,—as you say it will not,—I will give you the three hundred dollars.'' Major Parish had his good rifle, well loaded, in his hand.

Poor Oytes could not hide his terror. He

cringed and squirmed to get away; but Egan made him stay there before the Major, and as soon as Oytes could speak, he said to the interpreter: "I am wicked, wicked; beg the good agent not to kill me! I will work and I will never give him and Egan any more trouble." And as long as Major Sam Parish was Uncle Sam's agent at Malheur, Oytes kept his word.

In the fall of 1874, I came to command the department within which was Malheur. With Captain Sladen, my aide, and my daughter Grace (a young lady of seventeen), I rode in a spring-wagon drawn by mules the forty miles from old "Camp Harney," via Malheur City, to the Malheur Indian agency. It was then a rough sage-brush country, with very few houses and settlements. I remember how terrified my daughter was at the tavern in Malheur City on account of the noise and disturbance of drunken white men.

267

At the agency, Mr. Parish and his good wife, aided by Sarah, the interpreter, made us very welcome and comfortable. In the night the Indians had a noisy dance lasting many hours. I heard the sounds, and they seemed to me as wild and frightful as the Apache war-dances which I had witnessed some years before. Uneasy in mind and sleepless, I rose about midnight and dressed, visited the agent and inquired what was the matter. Parish laughed and sent for Chief Egan and Sarah. "Oh," said the chief, "we were all so happy that General Howard had come and had brought the young lady, his daughter, that we had to celebrate the event by a good feast and dance." I was satisfied and happy to let the feast and the dance go on, so returned to my comfortable bed and was able to sleep without any further interruption till morning. My intimate friends always teased me about that experience and asked: "What were you afraid of at Malheur?" I answered, "My alarm was simply from superstition based on ignorance!"

Early the next morning I visited the agent's office and had an interview with Chief Egan, Oytes, and several leading Indians. I noticed then how superior Egan was to the others. He had on an ordinary farmer's suit of light linen duck with a leather belt around his waist, a sheath holding a sheath-knife by his side. He wore a straw hat that he removed when he spoke to me. He had all the features of a full-blooded Indian, but wore no braid or ornament. His hair, parted in the middle, was cut short at the neck. His pleasant face and resonant voice were mainly used, that morning, in praising Major Sam Parish, and in telling me how grateful all the Indians were that the Great Father had sent them such an honest agent and good friend. The Indians had been roaming and wild and had never had a school before for the numerous children. Now they had a beautiful school and a mother teacher whom all the little ones loved; Mrs. Parish, the teacher, and Sarah, the interpreter, made all this very plain to me.

In 1877 I had a long-drawn-out trouble with Chief Joseph and his Nez Percés, from May till November. Buffalo-Horn, a war-chief, brought me from Idaho about a dozen of his Bannocks to help my soldiers as scouts. The Piutes under Chief Egan also refused to help my enemies, so remained at Malheur and improved their land and raised good crops upon many acres of it.

Sometimes during my long march in pursuit of Joseph—a march of over 1400 miles—Buffalo-Horn became dissatisfied with my officers and myself because we would not let him kill two friendly Nez Percés, and because I did not conduct the war to suit him.

On this account and for other causes, the next year, as soon as the bunch-grass became green and abundant, Buffalo-Horn and a body of Bannocks began a dreadful raid, coming west from the farthest eastern edge of my Department. As they came they stole horses and cattle and destroyed the houses and families of the white settlers in the usual wild Indian way. They forced to join them band after band of "Snakes," Columbia Indians, and Piutes; also took in scattered families of the Cayuses and Umatillas. At the Great Stein Mountain in southeast Oregon, some 400 miles from the place of starting, Buffalo-Horn's Indians under a new chief, for Buffalo-Horn had fallen in one of his battles with my soldiers, met and made an agreement with the Malheur Indians of Egan.

Before this, on the first of May, 1876, everything had been prosperous at Malheur,

271

—the children all at school and the fields already planted, and the ditches to bring water to the gardens well laid out and dug, and store-houses and stables constructed. The Indians, old and young, with scarcely an exception, were well and contented.

But toward the last of the month, Major Parish called the people to the school-house and then amid a great silence he said: "I have received a letter from our Big Father in Washington saying another man is to come here in my place. You must do just as he wants you to do. Go right along just as you have done while I have been with you."

It was Rinehart who was coming. He had lived in Canyon City and many of the Indians knew him. They all were against the change of agents. Egan went to Colonel Green at Camp Harney and begged him to try to convince the Big Father to let Parish stay. I was written to and besought to stop the change if I possibly could. Egan and Oytes declared that Rinehart had sold many bottles of fire-water to the Indians. After the new agent came there was another talk.

Egan's speech at this time is on record. It is: "Our Father (meaning Rinehart), we cannot read; we don't understand anything; we don't want the Big Father in Washington to fool with us. He sends one man to say one thing, and another to say something else. Major Parish told us the land was ours, and what we raised on it would be ours. You say it is government land and not ours." Egan called Rinehart's attention to the work they had done, and to the cruelty of taking the land and the crops from them, etc., etc.

Rinehart at once became angry and said: "Egan, I don't care whether any of you stay or not. You can all go if you do not like the way I do!"

Next, all went to work, as the agent had

273

promised to pay in money every one who worked faithfully. At the end of the week they came to Rinehart's office for their pay. He at once estimated the value of blankets, coats, trousers, shoes, socks, woolen-shirts, handkerchiefs, looking-glasses, shawls, calico, muslin, sugar, tea, coffee, etc., etc. He was going to pay them in the things that Uncle Sam had already given them.

Egan then spoke again: "Why do you play with us? We are men and not children; but never say you are going to pay us in money, and then not do it! I do not care for myself, but my men want their pay. Pay them in money, and then they can go and buy whatever they like: our Big Father's goods are too dear. We can go to our soldier fathers and get better blankets than yours for half the price you charge."

Rinehart became more angry than before and said, "If you don't like my ways you can all leave here. I never allow a white man to talk as you have.''

The Indians went to their tepees to mourn and talk all night. Next day, to make matters worse, a band of Piutes came who were nearly starving. Rinehart curtly refused to give them a mouthful. The morning after, Rinehart saw a little boy who did not understand English innocently laughing; he seized him by the ear and kicked him till he cried aloud from pain; and he told the Indians that he must be instantly obeyed or he would treat them as he did the boy, who had not carried a message as he told him.

Oh, the misunderstandings and heartburnings of these poor people! Chief Egan and his best men appealed from the decisions of the Indian agent, but to no good result, for just then Uncle Sam was trying to make his red children work for all they had, and such an agent as Rinehart made their tasks as painful and difficult as possible. Hatred begot hatred, and all the Indians at Malheur in despair went off to live by hunting and fishing and gathering of herbs and fruits, as their people had always done.

Months after the Indians left Malheur and Rinehart, it was on Stein's Mountain that the Bannocks in their war-raid came upon hundreds of them. "Come, go with us," they said, "and we will beat the white soldiers, and conquer all the white settlers who have our lands, and be rich and no longer poor."

Chief Egan held out against war as long as he could get a hearing. The Indians put him aside and put Oytes at the head of the discontented of the Piutes for a time, but after long reflection and the saving the lives of several of his friends, whites and red men, Egan at last consented to be their war-chief. He commanded in several battles, but was never very successful. After the last battle

276

of the Piute and Bannock War had been fought, Egan's life was taken by Umapine, a Umatilla scout. Umapine was a cruel and wicked man, and did not live long after that action of his in the Blue Hills of Oregon.

Our surgeon, Doctor Fitzgerald, obtained from Umapine the head of Chief Egan and sent it as a fine specimen of an Indian head of large brain to the Medical Museum in Washington. The Piutes felt keenly this last and greatest humiliation that their much loved chieftain's head should have such a dreadful and ignoble resting-place. Egan lost his wife and two children in war, but a little one had remained till his death to comfort him.

All the white people and all the Indians spoke well of Chief Egan. He had often borrowed money and food of our officers, but always repaid what he borrowed. He was exceedingly kind to his niece and to his youngest child.

XVII

LOT, A SPOKANE CHIEF

THE Spokanes, when they were not off on a buffalo-hunt or camping here and there to store up the camass roots for winter as the squirrels store up beechnuts, used to live along the banks of the Spokane River in Washington State. This river, with many falls and rapids, flows through great forests west to the Columbia. It is a beautiful land of wooded hills and fertile valleys, and the Indians clung to it with great fondness. Here are found every sort of game. The deer run wild in the natural parks, and the speckled trout dart up-stream, shining in the creeks and rivulets.

There was an old bridge across the Spokane, and as I rode to Fort Colville, escorted by some cavalry, we saw an open field covered with Indian lodges just to our right as we came to the bridge. There were ten or twelve lodges and one hundred and twenty Indians. Many Indians came out to meet us on the road, and I called to one of them in English: "What Indians are these?" He replied: "A band of Spokanes." The leader of this band was Lot, and I must tell you about him.

Long ago, when Lot was a small boy, Mr. Eeles, a good teacher, came to live among the Spokanes, just as in 1840 the famous Dr. Marcus Whitman went to teach the savage Cayuses. The Indians called this teacher Father Eeles, and, although he died long ago, they still speak of him with affection, and white people name roads and hamlets for him. Father Eeles loved the little Indian boy who would be a chief some day, and he baptized him and called him Lot.

Now Lot had grown to be a fine, tall Indian

279

chief, over six feet in his heelless moccasins, and but for his braided hair and the blanket over his shoulders you would have taken him for an old hunter. He spoke very little English, and was very modest, but Mr. Campbell, the Indian agent, brought Lot to me at once, saying as he did so: "Lot is a splendid Indian. He became a Christian and has always tried to live as Father Eeles taught him." I took a fancy to Lot immediately and asked him why his band were here, and what they were doing, and he told me that one of his Indian girls was to become the wife of a squaw-man who lived in a house just beyond the bridge, and that the band had come to see Mr. Campbell marry them.

Now a white man who marries an Indian woman is called by every one a squaw-man, and always belongs half to the Indians and half to the white people. Lot asked if I would stay for the wedding, and I was only too glad to accept his invitation. The bride was a pretty Indian girl, just fourteen years old, and she came out of one of the lodges with some Indian women and her parents, grandparents, and brothers and sisters.

The squaw-man, Mr. Walker, was about forty years old, and a rather rough-looking man in shabby clothes. He came across the bridge with some fine-looking Indian braves, and I could not help wondering why the little Indian girl had not chosen one of them for her husband. But perhaps she thought it was grander to live in a house and be Mrs. Walker. At any rate, Mr. Campbell, after a short prayer, had them hold hands while he married them, and then all the Indians sang one of our hymns, but in the Spokane language. After the wedding we went on to Fort Colville, and the next time I saw Lot he asked me to come with him to a religious service. Spokane Williams, one of his band, had taken

land like a white man and built a house. To
be sure, it was a small house with one door
and no windows, but he was proud of it, and
here the Christian Indians met. There was
a platform at one end where we were to sit,
and Mr. Campbell was there too. All the
people sat on the hard earth floor, men, women, children, and papooses packed in like
sardines. This service was a preparation for
the commemoration of our Lord's Supper,
and all the Indians stood up and told what
they were sorry they had done. One big
fellow said that he had stolen four horses; but
afterward he was very sad and took them
back to the white man they belonged to, and
asked his forgiveness; so the white man said:
"All right, John," and then he was happy
again. A woman said she had told an un-
truth, but afterward she was so miserable she
had to go and ask to be forgiven. After a
while an old Indian woman got up and talked

for a while, but Lot stopped her and told her to sit down. I asked Mr. Campbell what they were saying, and he told me she had been finding fault with her neighbors, but the chief said: "You may tell us the wrong things you have done yourself, but you must n't tell us the bad things your neighbors have been doing." Lot was very careful to make the people of his band do what was right.

Now Spokane Garry was the head chief of all Spokane Indians, and he asked me to meet him at an Indian Council. Garry was a small, pompous, querulous old man, not at all like Lot. He spoke English very loud and very fast, and was hard to understand. What he wanted me to know was that the Spokanes had helped the white settlers much more than the Nez Percés, and he thought the great Father at Washington ought to treat them as well and give them a reservation, as good a one as the Nez Percés had.

I told him I wished his Indians would all build houses and take up land like white men. Spokane Williams of Lot's band had done so, and was doing well. But Garry stopped me and said that white men's ways were not Indians' ways. Indians liked to go from place to place and take their lodges with them. If they lived in houses they must stop in one place. I sent his request to Washington, but he died before there was any reply, and Lot became a leader and guide to all these people. I often saw Lot, and we had long talks about the Indians. He moved his people to a prairie land where there was good water and plenty of trees, and here I visited him and felt as safe among these wild people as I do in my own home. But Lot always said, as Garry did, that Indians could not live like white men. He told me that if he could keep them together the old men and women would work while the young men could hunt partridges, wild turkey, and deer, but if they tried to live as white men no one would work. Every time I saw Lot he talked in this way till I came to believe it was so, and when President Hayes and General Sherman came to Oregon I told them what Lot had said to me, and asked the President to give these Indians some land for their own. General Sherman agreed with me that this would be the best thing for everybody, and the President signed a paper ordering enough land to be set aside for all the Spokane people. So Lot had his wish.

Some months afterward, when the President sent me orders to leave Washington Territory and go to West Point, New York, Lot in his far-off reservation heard that I was going. He mounted his pony and with some of his braves rode three hundred miles to beg me to stay. He arrived in Portland, Oregon, just as I was going on board the ocean steamer, anchored in the Willamette River, which was to take me to San Francisco. Lot was too excited to speak much English, but he found his way to my state-room and, big giant that he was, took me in his arms as if I were a small boy, saying, "No, no! you not go! You stay here and we have peace!"

Of course I could not stay, and after a while Lot understood that where the President sent me I must go, but we parted as if we were indeed brothers, and this noble Indian went back to his tribe to teach them what was best in life and to continue his good work for his people.

XVIII

FAR away in Wyoming lived the Sioux Indians, a fierce and warlike tribe. They called themselves Dakotas; but their enemies said that when they fought they did everything in a mean, hidden way so that it was hard to know what to expect, and they called them Sioux, which means "snake-like-ones." To this tribe belonged a young brave who wanted very much to become a chief. His father was a fierce warrior and had taught him how to fight, but he was not satisfied to follow the leaders of his tribe, for he wanted to lead other Indians himself. When this young man was only eighteen years old he had already learned to use the bow, could ride Indian ponies and swim deep rivers, and was a great buffalo-hunter; besides, he often danced in war dances with older braves. In some way he managed to get a rifle which fired several times without reloading, and after that he began to feel of much more importance than other young Indians.

At first the young braves were angry with him, but he soon showed them that he was a skilful warrior, and before long many young Indians chose him for their leader. Now he could wear an eagle feather in his war bonnet, and was a real chief.

At this time Uncle Sam had promised to give each Indian a good blanket, and they were glad to get them. The blankets were all bright red, and when this young Indian and his followers, each wearing a red blanket, rode rapidly past, some one said, ''See the Red Cloud.'' From that time on the young leader was called ''Red Cloud,'' and so far as I know was never after given any other name.

288

An attack on a wagon-train by Red Cloud's Sioux warriors

RED CLOUD

The Sioux Indians have a wonderful festival which they call the sun dance. At this time all the braves try to show how much pain they can bear without flinching, and some people say it makes them tender-hearted. Certainly "Red Cloud" always could bear more than any other warrior, and yet his heart was fierce and warlike. In time the Indians came to fear him, and little by little he was chosen war chief of all the wild Dakotas or Sioux. He hated the white people, and when other Indians tried to make peace Red Cloud always said: "No; war, war!" Perhaps he knew that just as soon as there was peace he would no longer be a chief, at any rate, he would not listen to any plan to stop fighting.

Fort Phil Kearny in Wyoming was in the middle of the Indians' country. One day word came to the major there that a party of soldiers who had gone to get firewood had been attacked, and some were killed, the rest in great danger. The major at once sent out a rescue party under Captain Fetterman, but Red Cloud was waiting with two thousand warriors, and not one white man escaped.

Nobody could say now that Red Cloud was not a great leader, and even Uncle Sam, however much he feared him, had to confess that he was "Chief of all the living Sioux Indians." All the Sioux chiefs whose fathers had been chiefs before them were willing to give some Indian lands to the white people and live on a reservation, but Red Cloud said: "No, no; I want war," and the young warriors followed him in spite of the chiefs. He had many battles and would not stop fighting.

At last, in 1874, the Indians came to one of Uncle Sam's army posts for a "big talk." A Christian gentleman opened the talk with a prayer, and when he finished Red Cloud said that the Indians prayed to the Great Spirit too, so he would pray. Then he asked the Great Spirit to forbid the white men taking away the Indians' land, and from wickedly destroying their homes where they and their fathers had lived for years and years. It was a wonderful prayer, and when Red Cloud sat down, every one kept very still, for they did not know what to say. Well, after the big talk, the Indians agreed to give up the land they had fought for, and went to live on what was called "Red Cloud Reservation." But still peace did not come. They were always ready to break out, and every once in a while houses were burned, stages waylaid, and people killed. It was no use to wish for peace so long as Red Cloud wanted war.

At last, after many years, the war chief began to feel that he could not win his fight, so very sadly he buried his tomahawk and signed what he called "a peace paper." But he did not really love his white brothers, and when Uncle Sam wanted Indian scouts to help him fight in 1876, Red Cloud was angry, and sent some of his warriors to waylay the soldiers and Indian scouts. Then Uncle Sam said that Red Cloud could not expect to be a chief if he did such things, for the officers found that he was always planning to make trouble, and they put Spotted Tail, a chief who was frank and honest, in Red Cloud's place. But what good did that do when the young Indians loved Red Cloud and did what he said? And he kept them from working with their hands, and said braves must only hunt and fight, and would not try to keep peace or help Spotted Tail.

Then at last, when Red Cloud was a very old man, more than eighty years old, he was sick for the first time in his life. He had to stay in his lodge and be taken care of, for he was too weak to move. Now he began to no-

Red Cloud

tice how kind every one was to him when he could do nothing for himself, and his heart was softened. When he was able to be up again and to go out into the woods, he was very happy, and began to be sorry for people who were not strong and well, though before he was sick he had always despised them.

He saw how Uncle Sam was trying to take care of everybody in this big country of ours, and he said, "Indians must take land like white men, they must work with a plow and hoe, and they must read books and study." Then there was peace in the north land, for the fiercest of all our Indian warriors had really surrendered.

XIX

TWO of our States, as boys and girls know from their geography, are called Dakota,—one North Dakota, the other South Dakota, and this was also the name of Indian people of different tribes speaking the same language, who lived in the country north of the great Platte River, and between and along our two greatest rivers, the Missouri and the Mississippi. The word Dakota means united by compact, and there were several united tribes who called themselves the *Dakotas*.

Sitting-Bull was a Dakota Indian. He was born near an old army station, Fort George, on Willow Creek, and his father was

Jumping-Bull. The Indian chiefs are very fond of giving boys new names when they begin to do something which their friends notice. If a boy runs fast with his head up, they call him "The Elk," "The Deer," "The Wild Horse," or some such name. Or perhaps if he has quick or sly ways, they name him "The Fox," "The Wolf," or "The Coyote."

In North Dakota, at this time, there were great herds of buffalo,—and the largest of them were the bulls. These were the leaders when a herd was running, swimming a river, or jumping across a gully. Even when a lad, Sitting-Bull's father could hunt for buffaloes, and quickly jump the deep gullies so frequent in that country, always with his bow in his hand, so his uncle, an Indian chief, named him Jumping-Bull.

His son was a strange boy. His hair was straight like an Indian, but of a reddish-brown color. His head was very large and his features were more regular in form than that of the Indian. He was so odd in his looks and his ways, keeping much by himself, thinking and planning how best to have his own way, that his father named him when quite young, "Sacred Stand."

Once, at ten years of age, he went with some hunters on a wild chase for buffaloes and came back to his father's wigwam very happy and proud, for he had succeeded in killing a buffalo-calf; but he did not have a new name till four years later. Then he waylaid an Indian, an enemy of his people, and shot him with an arrow. As soon as he saw that his foe could never rise again, he crept up to his head and cut off the top portion of the skin with the hair belonging to it. This "scalp," about as large as a silver dollar, he tied to his belt and carried to his home, full of joy and triumph, for he was now a *Brave* among braves. After this he frequently made drawings of his *totem,* what we might call his family coat-of-arms. This was a buffalo-bull settled back on his haunches in a sitting posture, and from it the boy was named "Sitting-Bull."

His second great feat was when he met a Crow Indian traveling along a trail claimed by the Dakotas. The Crow Indian was riding a horse, and had by his side, on another horse, his wife, with a baby strapped to her back. Sitting-Bull, on an Indian pony, charged this little cavalcade, succeeded in killing all three without getting a scratch, and made a rough picture of the exploit which he showed to his young companions.

Chief Red Cloud had led the Indians in 1868 at the time when a large number of our men fell in battle near Fort Phil Kearny, and after that trouble a scout picked up an old roster-book which had once belonged to a company of our soldiers. On its blank pages Sitting-Bull had made skeleton pictures, and each picture showed some wicked deed. The pictures were ridiculous enough, but they made a fairly good diary, and the meaning could not be mistaken. Nearly every record in the book was a sketch of Sitting-Bull and his victims. Sometimes he was killing white men, sometimes Indians, sometimes stealing and driving off herds of horses. A man's figure with a tall hat was enough to mean a white citizen, an uncouth bonnet showed a woman, stiff outlines gave Indian war feathers or a soldier's costume, and the book was a curious record of years when Sitting-Bull was a famous brave and a cruel, bad Indian.

Uncle Sam was greatly disturbed about "The Black Hills" of South Dakota at this time. Some white men, roaming through the hills, found signs of gold. They began to dig up the surface of the ground in many spots and to make deep holes and were sure there were large mines of gold there. The Dakotas insisted that these Hills all belonged to them. But the white men said that the Indians did not own "the whole earth," and tried hard to have the Indians sent away. This made Sitting-Bull very angry. He hated the white men more and more. He brought together thousands of Indians who were full of discontent and wanted to drive all white men from their country. A new band of Indians he formed and named "Strong-hearts." These he brought from eight or ten tribes of the Dakotas to a queer place in Montana, called "The Bad Lands." There were such deep gullies in clayey soil all around that neither horses nor buffaloes could leap over them, and this was Sitting-Bull's stronghold. He, himself, did not often go out to battle, for he was a medicine-man, not a warrior.

303

He would shut the flaps of his wigwam and stay hours, and sometimes days, inside, doing what he called "making medicine." He told the Indians that a powerful Spirit came to him at such times and gave him knowledge and orders.

He had influence with the wildest Indian chiefs because they had a strange fear of medicine-men. They thought him a great prophet and teacher; with their bravest soldiers they went out from the Bad Lands as from a great fort, when he told them to, and fought many successful battles with our men.

At last in 1876 General Terry, General Crook, and General Gibbon, with forces, from three different directions marched against Sitting-Bull and his "hostiles," who, about that time, came down from the Bad Lands and camped in four or five large villages with men, women, and children. His own village was near the middle of the great multitude

of wigwams. He declared that he had had a
dream—vision, and that he had seen in the
vision soldiers coming. This soon came true
and first came General Crook's troops from
the south, but the Indians were so many the
general stopped and waited for more soldiers.
Next came some of Terry's and Custer's men
from the east. The Indians were now much
excited, the women and children were hurried
off westward to safer grounds, and the warriors rushed pell-mell to meet the soldiers.
The Indians wounded many, killed many,
and drove the rest to the bluffs above the
Little Big Horn River.

After this Sitting-Bull in his wigwam,
"making his medicine" and talking to the
Spirit, heard the news of General Custer's
rapid charge up the slopes toward the villages, and all Indian warriors say he was
dreadfully afraid. He had his "Strong-
hearts" all around him, but his own heart

305

did not remain strong. They say as soon as he heard that "Long-Hair" Custer was coming fast and furious, in great haste he took his family, mounted them on ponies, and, jumping upon his own horse, galloped to the west, till he had reached a place of safety. Now he sent out many Indian warriors, ten to one, against Custer's brave men, and the Indians got around them and fought till not one soldier was left alive after the great battle called "Custer's Massacre." But Sitting-Bull was miles away. After a time he returned to his village because he had missed one of his twin-children, and when he reached his wigwam he found the child that he so much loved. The sounds of battle grew less and less and the conflict was over, but Sitting-Bull lost the good-will of his big chiefs because he was not there to share the danger and direct them when the storm was fiercest. His followers named the twins in fun "The-

One-Taken," and "The-One-Left," and they
long lived to remind the Indians of their
father speeding away from his greatest battle-field.

After the battle the whole United States
Army was sent to break up the Indian strong-
holds in and near the Bad Lands. The ablest
warrior chiefs, Gall, Spotted Eagle, Lone
Wolf, Lame Deer, and Crazy Horse were at
last killed or conquered. And it was not
long before Sitting-Bull and his "Strong-
hearts," full of hatred and discontent, fled
across the Canada line, where they were safe
from attack. The other Indians who had
fought and been beaten now went to the nearest Indian reservation, and for a time there
was peace among the Dakotas.

At last Sitting-Bull succeeded in getting back to the Grand River in North Dakota, where he had a rough, but comfortable,
house with some of his family. But it was

not long before the wide-awake Indian Agents and officers of the army found that Sitting-Bull was sending messages from camp·to camp and getting ready for another defiance of Uncle Sam's great army. They heard of ghost dances, but the real danger was from the plans of Sitting-Bull, plotting and mapping out another fearful outbreak of savage Indians.

In December, 1890, General Ruger was commanding the department of Dakota. He was living at St. Paul, Minnesota, where were his headquarters. Here he heard that Sitting-Bull was fretful, sullen, and secretly reorganizing the "Strong-hearts." Then General Ruger telegraphed the commander at Fort Yates, near Standing Rock, to have Sitting-Bull arrested. The Indian Agent asked it as a favor that his forty Indian policemen might make the arrest. They proceeded to his lodge, found him asleep, awak-

"He came out wild with anger"

ened him, and forced him to come out. He came out wild with anger and called for his warriors to join him; one of the Indian policemen took his gun and ran toward Sitting-Bull. Then firing began. Bull-Head, the chief of the policemen, was shot in the leg. He turned and fired at Sitting-Bull and other policemen did the same. Sitting-Bull did not live to speak another word, but the warriors kept fighting till the soldiers, near at hand, rode up and put an end to the affair.

To look at Sitting-Bull one would say that he was always quiet and self-contained. In fact he did usually keep himself under control; but he was cruel and almost heartless. He had practised cruelty to animals and men from his childhood, and as long as he lived; he was full of passion, and often very angry. He was always imperious and insolent toward our generals, the Indian Agent, and other friends of the Great Father at Washington,

311

whom he claimed to hate. He had great talent and ability to plan campaigns and battles, wonderful influence in bringing them together, and mostly the discontented and criminals of every tribe of his nation flocked to his standard. Notwithstanding all this, as if conscious of a wicked heart and fearing some punishment, he was afraid of death, and always terrified when defeat stared him in the face. Though he planned the greatest victory which the Indians ever gained over white men, Sitting-Bull himself was a coward, and disgraced himself even before his own people by running away in the very face of success.

XX

THE Shoshone Indians lived long ago in the Rocky Mountains, but they have gradually moved westward until now they live on the western side, where there are two wonderful springs which send water eastward and westward to flow into our two great oceans. The water from one flows through the Yellowstone Park to the Missouri River, and then by way of the Mississippi and the Gulf of Mexico to the Atlantic Ocean; while the other one flows westward into the Snake River and follows its many windings till at last it joins the Columbia, and after passing

313

the cascades, flows smoothly for one hundred and fifty miles till it reaches the Pacific Ocean.

Because these Indians live along the banks of the winding Snake River they are sometimes called "Snakes," but Shoshone is their Indian name.

As long ago as 1836 Washington Irving tells us that Captain Bonneville met Shoshone Indians on his way to the Pacific Coast. Even then the chiefs came together, smoked the peace pipe, burying their tomahawks and made up their minds to be good, peaceable Indians.

A tribe of Indians usually takes its character from the head chief. If he is a man who cares for his people, thinks for them, and leads them, then they follow and do what he says.

Washakie was such a chief, and his people loved and followed him. He had a large country, four hundred miles square, called the Wind River Reservation, and here he grouped his Indians in small villages about a beautiful spring of hot water which always flowed. At his request Uncle Sam had an army post near by, and for many years Washakie had chosen to be the friend of the white man.

Washakie was a tall, big man with fine eyes and a great deal of hair. He spoke broken English, but could make himself understood. He was a great eater, and it was always a mystery to me how one Indian could eat so much. He ate very politely, but it was like a giant taking his food. Washakie said: "I like meat, I like bread, I like vegetables; I am big, so I eat much." And indeed he did, enough for two or three white men. He was a great buffalo-hunter, and usually wore a fox-skin robe which was very becoming to him, but before he sat down to eat he always took off this outer fur coat, which he did not need except in the open air.

The country where these Indians lived was very cold indeed. One of the stage-drivers, John Hanson, always tied shawls around his legs before he started on a trip, and he told me once that Bill Snooks, who drove the stage before he took it, froze both his legs when it was thirty degrees below zero, and that was nothing unusual; so the Indians were glad to wear furs to keep them warm.

Now there was a great deal of gold in the mountains where these Indians lived, and Sioux, Shoshones, Cheyennes, Crows, and others all agreed to sell their land, which was valuable for mining, to our government, and go where there was no gold, but good water and plenty of game.

"Washington" agreed to pay the Indians for their land, and they moved away as they had promised, but the money did not come.

"He told me of his latest battle"

The Indians all around Washakie had been sometimes friends to the white men and sometimes not, but when the money did not come they were ready to fight. They said: "You white men do not keep your promises." Washakie was the only one who seemed to understand that Washington was far away, and that the money must be voted by Congress before it could be paid. He would not fight, so the other Indians were angry with him, and a band of Crows attacked Washakie and his Indians. Now Washakie was a friend to white men, but he met the Crows in battle, drove them northward, and they were glad to run away as fast as they could, leaving their lodge poles behind them; so you see he could fight when he had to.

I often met this good Chief and we were fast friends. Once when I went through the Yellowstone Park he told me of his latest battle. The Sioux Indians had been determined to break the power of the Shoshones, to defeat them in battle, and carry them off captive. Led by young Red Cloud, the son of the famous war chief, a band of Sioux came upon Washakie, but he had so drilled his men that they held every pass through the mountains, and fought so hard that the Sioux were obliged to give up, particularly as their young chief, Red Cloud, fell in the last attack. Washakie received praise from the Indian department for the ability with which he kept his Indians together, and the help he gave our officers and soldiers.

He was always glad to see me, and in the Yellowstone Park sent Shoshone Jack with a band of Indians to ride just out of sight on all sides of us as a guard. We were as safe in that wild country with them around us as we would have been anywhere else in America.

When Washakie was old, and his hair was very white, his eldest son, Washakie, was killed, not in battle but in a drinking-place. Some one gave him whisky, and when he was drunk he had a fight with a white man and was killed. Then the old Chief Washakie covered his head and refused to be comforted. He said: "My Indians have always been good. They are not lazy like the Arapahoes who drink whisky. [The Shoshones have a great contempt for the Arapahoes.] And my son is dead. For him to die in battle would have made me sad, but for him to die like an Arapahoe Indian breaks my heart." For a long time he grieved, and ever afterward kept his head covered to remind himself and his friends of his deep sorrow, not because his son was gone, but because he had passed away in disgrace, as no Shoshone Indian should, to the Spirit Land.

XXI

HOMILI, the chief of the Walla Wallas, lived in two places: a part of each year on the Umatilla Reserve with the Umatillas, Cayuses, and other Columbia River Indians who were willing to stay there with the government agent; and part of the year, indeed, the greater part of it, at what he called his home just above the steamboat landing near the hamlet of Wallula.

On the Umatilla Reserve, Homili had good land, pasturage all around for his ponies, and a good farm-house. He could raise wheat and vegetables, too, in plenty when he could make his *tillicums* (children and followers) work for him. But Homili was lazy and shiftless, and just managed to say "Yes, yes," to the good agent, Mr. Cornoyer, and to keep a poor garden-plot, and let his many ponies run about with the herds of horses which belonged to other Indians. Homili was always fat and hearty, and he loved best his queer home just above Wallula. More than ten miles broad is the strip of sand and gravel along the Columbia on the south side above and below Wallula; the first time I saw Homili he met me at the steamboat landing. He had with him four or five very poorly dressed Indians, wearing very long, black, uncombed hair. Homili was dressed up for the occasion. He had on a cast-off army uniform buttoned to his throat, and an old stovepipe hat which had long since seen its best days. I wondered then how Homili could have found an officer's coat big enough for him, for while he was not a tall man he had so thickened up and broadened out that he looked shorter than he was. One of his tillicums could talk English a little and the miserable *Chenook* jargon a good deal. He called all food "mucky-muk," and used many queer words. He was the interpreter. Homili took me in at a glance: "Heap good. Arm gone. Tillicum's friend." Homili's interpreter so delivered to me his first message. I said I was glad to see Chief Homili. He and I would be friends!

Homili wheezed and stammered, while he laughed aloud. Homili always laughed. "Heap glad for such friend. Come over yon way and see my house and my tillicums. Homili has good heart, but poor house." Indeed his lodge, where torn canvas was flying in the wind about some crooked lodge-poles, and where squaws and children were hanging listless and idle near the opening, was a poor house. The wind was blowing as it always did near Wallula. The sky was clear and it was a bright, comfortable day in June. My aide, Captain Boyle, was with me, and we went on to Homili's lodge. He had around him without any order rough, poverty-stricken lodges or wigwams of different sizes and shapes. His people with straight, black, coarse, dishevelled hair, and ragged clothing to match, appeared to my inspection about as low and forlorn as any human beings I had ever seen. Cobblestones, thick in places, but usually scattered around, like potatoes spilled from a cart, were strewn on a foundation of sand, the surface of which every fresh breeze threw into the air. How could there be a more cheerless place to live in, where sage-brush had hard work to grow, and nothing what-ever could be planted with the least hope of a crop?

Homili had a rough bench beside his lodge. He motioned us to sit down while he stood with his Indian talker in front of us. As soon as he could get his breath after our quick walk, Homili said: "This home better for Chief Homili!"

"How is that, Homili?" I asked.

"Oh, Umatilla agent good man, but Umatilla Reserve makes Homili a slave. Here tillicums all free, laugh and play, shoot sagehens, fish in the river, do what they like. All his tillicums 'heap good'!"

I understood. "Anything more, Homili?" I inquired.

"Yes, Smoholly 's my friend, my priest. He dreams great dreams, and he tells all the Columbia Indians, miles and miles up and down the great river, about the Great Spirit; and often what 's coming. He cures sick folks by good medicine and drumming. He 's a great Indian—Homili's friend. Umatilla agent don't want my friend, says Smoholly makes trouble. Not so, he makes my heart glad!"

"Homili took off his tall hat and shook it at us"

That was all, and we parted good friends. He rode a small half-starved Indian pony to see me off on the little "strap railroad" that then ran eastward to Fort Walla Walla thirty miles away. From the back platform of the only passenger-coach Boyle and I waved our hats to Chief Homili, for he rode on the side of the train for half a mile. A good smart pony could have kept up with that strap-rail train all the way, but thin grass, very poor sage-brush, and the fat Homili riding, half the time, did not allow his pony either proper food or strength, so that the good-natured, jolly chief and his mount soon fell behind what the Wallula white people called the "burro-cars." Homili, losing the race, took off his tall hat and shook it at us for a good-by, and then turned back to the barren home of his choice. Two of his cross yellow Indian dogs, more like young wolves or fierce coyotes than civilized dogs, continued the race a while longer, hopping about near the engine and barking at the fireman who threw chunks of wood at them. At last they turned toward Wallula, dropping their tails behind them and looking at us as they passed for all the world as if they were ashamed of such a slow coach as ours. So ended my first visit with Homili.

The next time I came up the Columbia I stayed overnight at the Wallula Hotel, a funny tavern, where the partition-walls were as thin as laths. My friend the tavern-keeper always gave me a room situated, as he said, in the "bosom of the family," where I could hear everything that took place in all the house. I had hardly reached that lively inside room, when I was called to the office. "Two Indians want to see the General!" so the office boy called out at my door. On entering the office I met two Indian messengers with a white man called Pambrun. Pambrun had an Indian wife, and could talk several Indian languages. He lived ten miles from Wallula toward Walla Walla, and was much respected by whites and Indians. The Indian messenger's speech was brief and clear, for Pambrun put it in good English. They had paddled across the Columbia from Smoholly's village. He wanted General Howard, the new commander of the soldiers, to come over the great river and see him and his tillicums; they had come together from many tribes. His village was opposite the Homili Falls, above where the Snake River comes into the Columbia. I told Pambrun to tell the messenger to say to Smoholly that General Howard would remain the next day at Wallula, and that if Smoholly wished to see him during the day he could do so by coming to Wallula.

The rumor which troubled all the Indians of that up-country was that General Howard

331

had been ordered by the Washington President to put them all on the reservations to which they belonged.

The Indians went back to Smoholly with my message, but he was afraid to put himself in my power, because he was the head and front of all the lawless bands which went roaming over the country—Indians of whom the white settlers never ceased to be afraid. Then Pambrun sent Smoholly word that "Arm-cut-off" (the name Homili gave me) was a mild man and would do him no harm. Surrounded by a multitude of harem-scarem tillicums, men, women, and children, Smoholly, the next day, early in the afternoon, made his appearance at Wallula.

The tavern-keeper gave us the use of his tumble-down store-house, an immense building large enough for Smoholly and his four hundred red folks to crowd into. My aide, Smoholly, the Umatilla agent, Pambrun, and

I sat upon chairs perched on a long, broad box, which the tavern-keeper loaned us for a platform. It was a wild-looking set of savages down there that I looked upon, squatted upon the floor or standing by the back and sides of that roomy place. When Homili with a few followers came to honor our talk with his presence, I sent for another chair and seated him proud and laughing by my side. I took a long and searching look at Smoholly, and he did me a like favor, as if trying to read my thoughts. He was the strangest-looking human being I had ever seen. His body was short and shapeless, with high shoulders and hunched back; scarcely any neck; bandy legs, rather long for his body; but a wonderful head, finely formed and large. His eyes, wide open, were clear, and so expressive that they gave him great power over all the Indians that flocked to his village. That day Smoholly wore a coarse gray suit, somewhat

333

ragged and much soiled. Over his head was a breezy bandana handkerchief, two corners tied under his chin and the wind, coming through the cracks of the store, kept his head-cover in motion all the time.

Smoholly, who had asked me to come, was requested through Mr. Pambrun to tell General Howard what he and his followers wanted. Smoholly covered his face with both hands and remained in silence like a man praying; then commenced his talk, using short sentences. Pambrun translated each sentence into good English. "Smoholly heard that General Howard, a great chief in war, had come to command all the soldiers. He heard also that there was a new President in Washington. Indians call him Great Father. Major Cornoyer, the Umatilla Indian agent, sent messengers to Chief Homili, Chief Thomas, Chief Skimia, and to Smoholly with words: 'Come on the reservation.

HOMILI

All Indians come now. If you don't come before one moon, General Howard, obeying the
new President, will take his soldiers and
make you come to Umatilla or to some other
government reserve.' Smoholly, the Spirit
Chief of all the Columbia bands, who gives
good medicine, who loves right and justice,
now wants General Howard to tell Smoholly
the Washington law.''

I answered: ''I did not come to the Far
West to make war, but to bring peace. Major
Cornoyer has the law, he takes the law to the
Indians. We will listen to him.''

Major Cornoyer began: ''You all know I
am the Indians' friend; my wife is an Indian
woman, she is always your friend; the law is
for all the Indians to come on my reservation
or some other, there are many other reservations. Why not come without trouble?''

I said: ''Homili, I am sure, can answer that
question.'' Chief Homili hemmed and hawed,

wheezed and laughed, and at last began his speech.

"Homili and his tillicums to go to Umatilla Reserve! Cornoyer gives Homili leave to visit his home, the home he loves, right up there where the winds blow, where the sand flies, where the stones are piled up. Smoholly is our good friend and we like to see his face. Smoholly is wise and has a good heart. I am done."

I had no message from Washington, so I dismissed the council, saying I would write to the President what Smoholly, Major Cornoyer, and Homili had said. I was obliged to obey the President's law, and I think Smoholly would give good medicine if he taught all the Indians to obey the Washington law. The advice I gave worked well. Before September nearly all the Indians came to some reservation and were quiet for some time. Homili, too, stayed more on the Umatilla Reserve, but he and his pony made frequent visits to his wigwam among the stones of Wallula.

To keep the Indians contented, Cornoyer, helped by his Indian wife, induced Homili and six other Indian chiefs to visit Washington. My aide, Major Boyle, took charge of the Indian Delegation on the journey both ways. When some young hoodlums in San Francisco saw them walking along Sutter Street, they put their hands to their mouths and made as they thought an Indian warwhoop. Homili was somewhat frightened; he thought it might be a white man's war cry, and he had no weapon, not even a bow and arrows. He stammered and said, "Major Boyle, what 's that? Insult unarmed Indians! We treated you and General Howard better in Wallula. White folks—bad manners!"

On the overland railroad he liked most the

barren sands and long stretches of worthless country, better than cultivated fields, thriving villages, and prosperous cities. "Bad lands, you say; I like best, more like my sand and bushes on the Columbia."

Homili saw the "Great Father," but laughed and stammered too much to say anything except to Pambrun: "Tell the President that Homili always has a good heart."

Homili got very tired of Washington, and was homesick all the time. He kept saying: "Moucho tillicums" (too many people). His face brightened and his laugh had a happier ring when the steamer was going out of the Golden Gate into the great Pacific Ocean. Then Homili stammered: "Home, home!" His mind's eye was on the familiar scenes of the upper Columbia, and when the steamer had been a day or more at sea Homili caught sight of the shore two or three miles to the east and cried, "Oh, oh, stop this boat and let Homili go over there, he wants to walk!"

When I met the fat and jolly chief again he said: "You, General Howard, may like Washington, but," shaking his head with a disgusted frown, "Homili best likes his home by the Columbia River. Stones and sands and Indian tillicums always kind, make him happy there."

XXII

I HAPPENED to know a Umatilla scout who bore the English name of Cut-Mouth John. The Umatilla tribe of Indians to which John belonged lived along the upper waters of the great Columbia River. This country, called the "up-river country," is used also by the Cayuses, Walla Wallas, and other Columbia River Indians. There were many of them on the lands called reservations, and many others roaming about everywhere, far and near, like herds of wild horses on the great prairies of the West where there were no fences to stop them.

I was then living in Portland, Oregon, and all the soldiers in that part of the country

340

watered by the great western rivers, were under my command. I was to use the soldiers to keep peace all the time between the white inhabitants and the roaming red men. The whites were mostly farmers, cattle raisers, and shepherds, who had made their homes in all the rich valleys, along the streams of water, and on the beautiful hills and green slopes of the mountains. These people wanted all the good land to pasture their herds and flocks; and the red men wanted the same land for hunting and for feeding their ponies and for gathering for themselves things which grew without sowing or planting, such as camas, the wild onions, the berries, and the fruits of trees. There for many years the red men had found acres and acres of "bunch" grass which made their ponies lively and fat. But the white men, when they came, put up fences, bars, and gates. These

341

the red men, when they came along every spring, tore down and kept saying: "This land is ours. Our fathers had it before any white men came to this country."

"Uncle Sam" then sent Colonel Watkins from Washington to Oregon and to the "up-river country" to talk with the red men, and to settle the troubles which everywhere had sprung up.

I went with him on a large steamer up the Columbia. The steamer could go only to the Cascades. Here we changed to a train of cars for a few miles, going past some foaming rapids as far as Celilo. There we had a smaller steamer which bore us through smooth water forty miles to the Dalles, a small village near that part of the Columbia where it tumbles foaming and roaring over more narrow rocky rapids. People say the river here is "on edge." Colonel Watkins, Captain Wilkinson, and I crossed to the north

CUT-MOUTH JOHN

side of the Columbia and then went by rough
roads over a broad shaggy mountain. We
had with us an Indian chief, Skemiah, and
his son, eight years old. I had taken them
from prison and set them free upon Skemiah's promise of obedience to Uncle Sam's
laws in the future. When well over the
mountain we found the rich prairie, vast in
extent and covered with the pretty cabins of
the red men. It was called the Simcoe Reservation, and the agent, tall as Abraham Lincoln, was called Father Wilbur. So the red
men were named Simcoe Indians, the most
of whom looked like our farmers dressed in
clothing such as white men wear; but a few
in one corner of the reservation still had on
blankets and skins of animals. Father Wilbur called them Blanket Indians,—these few
were the restless roamers. Skemiah was
their chief, and they were happy to see him
again, and seemed more pleased when the

343

lad, his son, rode among them having on a pretty cap and a bright belt.

Colonel Watkins and Father Wilbur called in many red men far and near for a meeting, so that we had a "big pow-wow." Smoholly, Moses, Indian Thomas, One-Eyed John, Young Chief of the Umatillas, and his friend the famous scout, named Cut-Mouth John, came together to meet us and many Simcoe Indians near Father Wilbur's house; each chief had with him a few of his tribesmen.

It proved to be a great meeting; a council where white men and red men for two whole days spoke their minds to one another, and this gathering had the good result to keep nearly all the Indians who were north of the Columbia away from those terrible Nez Percés who were about to go on the war-path.

The next day after the council in a nice large wagon drawn by good-sized mules,

An Indian scout

Watkins, Wilkinson, and I, escorted by Chief Stwyre and several Simcoes mounted on ponies, went across the prairie, through the white settlements north of Simcoe, and then followed the sluggish Yakima River eastward for miles to its mouth, where it ran into the Columbia. Cut-Mouth John and two or three of Smoholly's men had come on with our escort. When the others, becoming weary, left us for their homes, they stayed with us all day. Smoholly had hastened on before us and crossed the broad Columbia in canoes before our arrival a little after sunset. Wilkinson became very ill. The mules and driver were too tired to go further. Wallula, the steamboat landing from which I must go up the Snake River to Lewiston to see the Nez Percés, was twenty miles below.

I thought I might go down the river in a small boat. At first the brave John and two red men offered to swim a half mile across the Columbia and get a boat, but I would not allow them to risk that. Then they gave the Indian "whoop" several times and when an answer came from the other shore they cried in Indian: "Send a boat for the white chiefs." Smoholly, across the river, had one made ready. After some delay two stalwart Indians could be heard paddling over what proved to be a long log dug-out, rather old and the worse for too much water soaking. Watkins and I ate our supper, Wilkinson being at first too ill to eat. We fixed a bed for him and placed him in the bottom of the dug-out. Cut-Mouth John took the steering paddle, and the other two crouched near the middle of the boat, paddling skilfully when necessary in the rapid river, while Colonel Watkins and I placed ourselves in front to watch the water, the shores, and the abundant stars in a cloudless sky. Pambrun, the inter-preter, enabled us to talk with the Indians, and helped when necessary to manage our strange craft. It was a very dangerous and exciting passage. We ran into many dark eddies, avoided the small islands, and coursed swiftly through the Homily Rapids, roaring frightfully,—enough to disturb our nerves.

As we passed the mouth of the Snake River we shot into smoother water with the wind— the current and the Indian paddles giving us the speed of a railroad train.

About two o'clock the next morning just as the dawn was appearing we reached the steamer landing at Wallula. The deck-hands were just ready to haul in the gang-plank when our strange boatload of people called to them. We were soon in safety upon the steamer's deck. Wilkinson had recovered from his illness, and as soon as possible ate a hearty breakfast with Watkins and myself in the steamboat galley.

349

Colonel J. W. Redington, who served as volunteer scout and courier for me during the Indian Wars, has told me several facts about the faithful scout, Cut-Mouth John, who brought us so skilfully to safety in the ungainly dugout. Cut-Mouth John was with our old officers long ago, campaigning in that upper country of the Snake River in pioneer days, and Redington thinks he was at a later period with General Sheridan in an Indian War in which the Simcoe Indians were against him. In one of those early wars, when the red men were trying to keep back the white men from taking their country, Cut-Mouth John was with our soldiers, became their friend, and remained with them all the time.

Once the Indians had made a fort on the Powder River, from which they believed that they could not be driven back. The scout John was a guide to our men. When he came near the fort he saw his own brother over there inside of the trenches, and he called to him with all his might to come out and leave those angry red men. But his brother said: "No, I will shoot you, John, if you come another step my way."

John was too brave to yield to his brother, so he led the charge upon the barricade. His brother kept his word and fired at him. The bullet only cut his lip or cheek, but disfigured him badly for life. The fort was captured and our soldiers praised John for his fearless conduct, and gave him the queer name.

Cut-Mouth John was one of my scouts in the beautiful Blue Mountains during the Piute and Bannock war of 1878, and he was again with Lieutenant Farrow when he captured the red men called "Sheep Eaters," a small tribe in the Salmon River Mountains in the year 1879. Cut-Mouth John was then an old man, but he was full of life, being the last man to roll himself up in his saddle-blanket at night, and the first one, long before sun-up, to turn out in the morning.

His only reward for all his faithful service to "Uncle Sam" was to be made an Indian policeman on the Umatilla Reservation with the poor pay of five dollars a month.

Once he came down to see me in Portland a short time before he passed over to the happy hunting grounds. He came in his soldier uniform to my office. "Who is this?"— I said gently, looking up.

"Don't you know me, General? I am your scout, 'Cut-Mouth John.'"

I am very, very sorry that the aged scout was neglected in his old age by the red men round about him. I am sure Uncle Sam would have done more for him had he known of his slim reward and poor, poor condition in those last days. He was a steadfast friend to the white men at all times, even to the end.

XXIII

FAR off in the Dragoon Mountains where Captain Red Beard took me to see Cochise in his stronghold, lived the chief of a band of Apache Indians, called Geronimo. His Indian name was Go-khlä-yeh, but after his first battle with the Mexicans he was called Geronimo, and the name was pronounced after the Spanish fashion, as if it began with an H instead of a G—Heronimo. When this Indian was a young man he went to Mexico to trade furs and beaded belts and moccasins for things the Indians use, and with him went his wife and many Indian men, women, and children. The Indian men made a camp near a small Mexican city and left the women and children there while they went into the town to trade, but while they were gone some white people fired at those left in camp, and when Geronimo came back all his family were dead, and everything he had was destroyed. At first Geronimo was so sad that he could not eat or sleep, and wandered about in the woods as unhappy as any one could be; then he began to be angry and wanted to fight all white men, and that is how he first made up his mind to go on the war-path.

Geronimo was a very quiet man and yet he danced with the other Indians, pitched quoits with them, or played the game of poles. This is called the pole fight. The Indians draw two lines on the ground twenty steps apart; then an Indian, taking a pole ten or twelve feet long, grasps it in the middle and, swinging it from right to left over his shoulders, runs from the first to the second line and casts the pole as far in front of him as he can. Geronimo was often the winner in games, for he played very well, especially a game called "Kah."[1]

This is always played at night and a great fire gives light for it. Sides are chosen with four on a side; one side they call beasts, the other side birds. An old blanket or piece of canvas is propped up between the beasts and birds and on each side they dig four holes and put a moccasin in each hole. Then one of the birds is chosen by lot and while all the birds sing he hides a small piece of white bone in one of the moccasins. The beasts have clubs, and when the blanket is suddenly pulled away one of them points with his club to the hole where he thinks the bone is. If he is right his side is given a stick from a bundle like

[1] For full description see "Geronimo's Life."

jackstraws held by an umpire. Those who win become birds and hide the bone. If they lose they remain beasts. When the jackstraws are all gone the game is over, and the side with most sticks wins.

Geronimo played games and danced, but all the time his mind was on war and he did not love his white brothers, so he lived in the mountains and planned battles. Often he had for his house a short, scrubby tree with a hollow in the ground near its trunk. Here he spread a deer-skin for his bed and some woolen blankets on a large stone close by for a seat. I am sure the friendly red men in the "Never, never, never Land," where Peter Pan lives, must have been Apache Indians, and that Peter Pan and the other boys learned from them to live in hollow trees. Perhaps Geronimo may have known Peter Pan, only I suppose he called him by some Indian name of his own. At any rate, this

Indian chief lived very often in hollow trees, and liked that sort of a home very much.

Geronimo was one of the Indian captains who was with Cochise when he decided that the Great Spirit wanted the Indians to make peace with the white men and eat bread with them. At that time most of the Indians were very happy to have peace, and Geronimo seemed quite as pleased as the others, though I believe he was not yet quite sure that it was time for peace to come. At any rate the great Cochise said it was, so Geronimo was ready to ride with us to meet the soldiers, and, as I was willing, he sprang up over my horse's tail and by a second spring came forward, threw his arms around me and so rode many miles on my horse. During that ride we became friends and I think Geronimo trusted me, although he trembled very much when we came in sight of the soldiers near Camp Bowie.

Most of the Apache Indians kept peace fairly well after that, but the white people and Mexicans were not good to them, and Geronimo did not love his white brothers, so he was on the war-path again before long.

Then Uncle Sam sent one of his officers to fight against Geronimo and his Indians, and they were made prisoners of war and taken far away from Arizona to the Mount Vernon Barracks in Alabama. Here they were fed and clothed and guarded. Their children were sent to school and they were all treated kindly, but they were prisoners and could not go away.

In 1889 I went to Mount Vernon Barracks, and the first man I saw as I got out of the train was Geronimo. He had a bundle of canes of different sorts of wood, which he had peeled and painted and was selling them one by one. When he caught sight of me he passed his canes to another Indian and ran to

"We came in sight of the soldiers near Camp Bowie"

meet me. I could not understand his Apache, but he embraced me twice and called his Mexican name, "Geronimo," "Geronimo," many times so that I should be sure to know who he was. Then he got an interpreter and came to talk with me. "I am a school superintendent now," he said. "We have fine lady teachers. All the children go to their school. I make them. I want them to be white children." From among the Indians at Mount Vernon Barracks there were formed two companies of soldiers, each of fifty Indians. Geronimo was very proud of them and kept saying, "Heap big! Tatâh; heap good!" and he told them to do their best to keep their uniforms bright and clean, to make their gunbarrels shine and never have dust on their shoes. But though Geronimo tried his best to be happy and contented, he was homesick for Arizona and begged me to speak to the President for him. "Indians sick here," he said,

361

"air bad and water bad." I told him that there would be no peace in Arizona if the Indians went back to the Chiricahua Mountains, for the Great Father at Washington could not control the Mexicans and white people there and make them do what was right; and Geronimo tried to understand. He still helped the teachers and stayed, himself, much of the time with the children to help keep order, but though he was doing his best to make his own people better, still he did not love his white brothers.

Geronimo was taken to the Omaha and Buffalo Expositions, but he was sullen and quiet, and took no interest in anything. Then at last all the Apache Indians were sent west again to the Indian Territory near Fort Sill, Oklahoma Territory, and here Geronimo began to go to church and became a Christian Indian.

The last time I saw him he was at the St.

Louis Exposition with the "Wild West Show." He stayed in St. Louis for several months, for people wanted to see him as much as they did the Filipinos from Manila, the Boers from South Africa, or the Eskimos from Alaska, and hardly any one went away without asking to see Geronimo, the great Apache war chief. His photographs were in great demand, and he had learned to write his name, so he sold his autographs and made a good deal of money. He wanted to see other Indians, too, especially Indians who were not Apaches. He was very much interested in other people from all over the world, the strange things that showmen did, the animals he had never seen before— bears from the icy north, elephants from Africa, learned horses, and other things new and strange. Nothing escaped him, and everything he saw was full of interest to him. Since he had become a Christian he was trying to understand our civilization and, at last, after many years, Geronimo, the last Apache chief, was happy and joyful, for he had learned to try and be good to everybody and to love his white brothers.